Refocusing on the Common Good:

Advancing Equity and Access in Higher Education

A Report on the College Board Colloquium

Refocusing on the Common Good:

Advancing Equity and Access in Higher Education

A Report on the College Board Colloquium

January 8–10, 2005
Bal Harbour, Florida
College Board, New York, 2005

The College Board: Connecting Students to College Success

The College Board is a not-for-profit membership association whose mission is to connect students to college success and opportunity. Founded in 1900, the association is composed of more than 4,700 schools, colleges, universities, and other educational organizations. Each year, the College Board serves over three and a half million students and their parents, 23,000 high schools, and 3,500 colleges through major programs and services in college admissions, guidance, assessment, financial aid, enrollment, and teaching and learning. Among its best-known programs are the SAT®, the PSAT/NMSQT®, and the Advanced Placement Program® (AP®). The College Board is committed to the principles of excellence and equity, and that commitment is embodied in all of its programs, services, activities, and concerns.

For further information, visit www.collegeboard.com.

Contents

Welcome and Opening Remarks

YOULONDA COPELAND-MORGAN, associate vice president of admission and financial aid, Harvey Mudd College, and chair of the College Scholarship Service Council (CSSC), opened the colloquium by welcoming everyone to sunny Florida. She said, "This is a wonderful way to start the new year, and I thank you for being here. Once again, the planning committee has put together a wonderful theme and recruited a variety of talented speakers and presenters to help us think more deeply about how we might refocus on the common good of higher education." The audience gave a round of applause in advance to the presenters from whom they would hear during the colloquium. Copeland-Morgan then introduced the members of the colloquium planning committee:

William Boyd, associate vice president, student services and budget administration, San Diego State University

Steven Brooks, executive director, North Carolina State Education Assistance Authority, and member of CSSC

Linda Dagradi, director of guidance, Longmeadow High School

Georgette DeVeres, associate vice president of admissions and financial aid, Claremont McKenna College, and chair of the Board of Trustees, the College Board

Mary Nucciarone, assistant director of financial aid, University of Notre Dame, and chair of the CSSC Financial Aid Standards and Services Committee (FASSAC)

Shirley Ort, associate provost and director of scholarships and student aid, University of North Carolina at Chapel Hill, and chair-elect of CSSC

Michael Scott, director of scholarships and financial aid, Texas Christian University

Joellen Silberman, dean of enrollment, Kalamazoo College

William Wells, director of financial aid, Wake Forest University, and member of CSSC

They were hailed with a round of applause from the audience. Copeland-Morgan praised the group for developing a program schedule that balances new research and current models around this year's theme. She then introduced Deb Thyng Schmidt, who would be writing up the proceedings; and Anne Sturtevant, director, financial aid solutions, the College Board, and Jim Miller, dean of admissions and financial aid, Bowdoin College, who would be serving as colloquium moderators and discussion facilitators. She concluded by thanking Linda Peckham, director of training and communications, the College Board, and Robin Casanova, program associate, the College Board, who were also greeted with a round of applause.

Next, Andre Bell, vice president, College and University Enrollment Services, the College Board, extended an official welcome to the participants on behalf of the College Board. "This is our tenth colloquium, hard as that might be to believe. Our theme this year covers timely topics and comes on the heels of a year of focus on these topics, with the celebration and professional development programs that were part of the fiftieth anniversary of the College Scholarship Service® and the launching of the College Board's diversity law and enrollment management collaboratives, focusing on student aid issues. This year, we will begin a collaborative on college recruitment outreach. So this colloquium is the capstone to a year of focus on challenges that are as old as our democracy itself."

He continued, "We hope you find the colloquium to be informative, inspiring, and thought-provoking as well as an opportunity to take home ideas for practical application on your campuses. Traditionally, the colloquium has provided the opportunity for a broad look at the issues just before we go back and dive headlong into the admissions and aid cycle. The colloquium is truly a function of the *membership* of the College Board, and I thank you in advance for your participation, questions, and advice for next year. And I hope you'll leave fully engaged in the pursuit of our democratic ideals of equity and access, which have proven so elusive."

Keynote Address:

The "Supply-Side Block" in Higher Education: Attainment, Equity, and Social Class

EUGENE TOBIN, program officer in higher education for the Liberal Arts College Program at the Andrew W. Mellon Foundation, gave the keynote address. He praised the planning committee for choosing the topics of equity and access, which are important issues for the country's future and subjects of growing interest among policymakers and the general public. He began, "The editors of *The Economist* recently observed that the United States likes to think of itself as the very embodiment of a meritocracy, and that most Americans believe that their country does a reasonable job of providing opportunities for everybody. . . . Yet the education system they observe is increasingly stratified by social class, and poor children have a double disadvantage: they attend public schools with fewer resources than those of their richer contemporaries, and America's great universities, according to *The Economist*, are increasingly reinforcing— rather than reducing—these educational inequalities."

Tobin went on to outline contemporary attitudes toward, and concerns about, higher education. "A 2004 survey found that 93 percent of respondents consider our colleges and universities to be one of the country's most valuable resources. But survey respondents are much more ambivalent about how and to whom access to these valuable resources should be provided. A robust majority worry that colleges are simply too expensive. Many parents expressed concern about being able to afford their children's education."

He indicated that, in terms of admissions measures that are nonobjective, 75 percent of those surveyed disapprove of legacy admissions, and the response to affirmative action was evenly divided. "There has long been a simmering debate in this country over whether it is better to educate a small number of people to a very high standard, or to extend educational opportunities much more broadly—even if this means accepting a somewhat lower standard of performance and spreading resources more thinly."

Tobin went on to describe what has been an even more pointed debate over efforts to admit students from a wide variety of cultural, socioeconomic, and religious backgrounds. In the early nineteenth century, poor, rural, young New England men sought a college education and worked their way through the "gentlemen colleges" on their way to enter the ministry and other emerging professions. During the 1820s and 1830s, the education of women became a controversial subject—first in women's academies and seminaries, then in women's colleges, and finally in coeducational institutions. In the late nineteenth and twentieth centuries, higher education leaders manipulated admissions policies to adjust to the influx of immigrant students from southern and eastern Europe by limiting the number of Jewish or Catholic students they would admit. And segregation, formal and de facto, served to limit the number of African American students who attended college.

"But today's barriers to entry are vastly different. Although explicit policies to keep certain people out have been eliminated, more organic barriers—such as poor academic and social preparedness, information deficits, and outright financial hardship—are limiting college opportunities for students from socioeconomically disadvantaged backgrounds: a group that contains more white students than minority students, although minority students are disproportionately represented." Tobin suggested that these barriers are in many ways more difficult to overcome than the barriers presented before.

Tobin described today's challenges. "Overall, college enrollment rates have increased for all racial, ethnic, and socioeconomic groups over the last three decades. Increases in real income, in student aid, and in the economics returns to higher education have combined to produce this very welcome result." But Tobin warned that the fact that these rates have gone up does not mean that there is equal access. According to the College Board's *Trends in College Pricing* (2003), an individual's chances of going to college are still closely correlated with family background and a host of factors related to college preparedness.

Students from high-income, educated families have enjoyed persistent advantages since the time they were young and, when college approaches, are encouraged to take college-preparatory classes and prepare for standardized tests. Students from wealthy families are far more likely to take the SAT® than students from lower socioeconomic strata, and are more likely to do much better on the tests. National Education Longitudinal Study (NELS) data demonstrate that students from the highest socioeconomic status (SES) quartile are six times more likely to score over 1200 than those in the bottom quartile of income; the figure is seven times higher for top-income quartile students than for those from the bottom-income quartile who are also the first in their family to attend college.

Tobin indicated that the fact that many low-SES high school graduates are qualified for college but do not attend—or attend colleges that are less selective than their achievements justify—is not widely recognized outside the higher education community. "The primary cause of this untapped resource is a 'supply-side block' that threatens this country's growth in educational attainment. The block exists in spite of rising economic returns to education. An academic preparedness gap starts at birth, continues through adolescence, and is shaped by students' in-school and out-of-school environments." Tobin indicated that the "inequities that dampen expectation" begin immediately and accumulate, from inadequate prenatal care to family instability, income disparities, unsafe neighborhoods, a lack of adult role models, underfunded educational programs, and the like.

The number of low-SES students who are prevented from attending college based on a straightforward inability to pay is actually quite small, according to research by economists Pedro Caneiro and Jim Heckman, who estimate that fewer than 8 percent of students nationwide fit this category. Tobin believes there is no question that higher income families have an easier time paying the bills, and that parents with higher educational attainment foster college attendance by providing advice, contacts, and encouragement. Tobin's research suggests that family finances have a fairly minor impact on a student's ability to attend college, in part because of the relatively low cost of less-selective institutions and the amount of financial assistance available at the more selective institutions. But "family finances are extraordinarily important" in developing students who are prepared for college; the pernicious effects of socioeconomic status make the educational opportunity gaps very hard to close.

According to Tobin, looking at differential graduation rates adds a level of complexity to a discussion of equity. In comparing high school graduates who started four-year college programs in 1992, there is a 34-percentage-point difference in bachelor's degree attainment between those in the top and those in the bottom-income quartiles. There is also a roughly 15-percentage-point gap in degree attainment between blacks and whites; this gap has not closed in 50 years. Although college enrollment rates are increasing, college completion rates are declining. Policies that encourage access for all but do not provide the guidance and resources to ensure degree attainment are, Tobin believes, a waste of public and individual resources. According to economist Sarah Turner, the private financial returns to a college degree retain to those who earn degrees, and those who attain them most quickly.

Tobin believes, "The progress of current students toward their degrees cannot be underemphasized. There is much to be said for allocating funds to those institutions that bear the brunt of rising enrollments. We should help them meet the legitimate educational needs of larger populations of students who may not be able to complete their degrees without considerable economic assistance. Why? The dictates of basic fairness suggest it's the right thing to do. But also, considerations of economic efficiency argue strongly for improving the college preparedness of marginal students, whose quest for a college degree may be frustrated *not* at the college door, but after they have passed through it."

Tobin moved on to discuss college choice. "There is no question that low-income students are underenrolling at our most selective institutions, even when we control for preparedness and other characteristics. Given the disproportionately high benefits that these institutions offer, this is a troubling finding." Tobin posed these questions: "Is it because the institutions are too expensive? Is it because these students are not up to the challenge? Are students from this group underapplying? Are they underadmitted?" Tobin shared data from a 19-institution (Figure 1) survey for the forthcoming book he has authored with William Bowen and Martin Kurzweil, *Equity and Excellence in American Higher Education*. Thanks to the College Board (which helped link the institutions' records to Student Descriptive Questionnaire data provided by SAT takers) and the institutions themselves, Tobin and his colleagues were able to analyze data from 180,000 applications to the institutions in 1995. "Should these highly regarded institutions be considered engines of opportunity or bastions of privilege?"

Figure 1: Number of Nonforeign Applicants and Enrolled Students, by Control and Institution, 1995 Entering Cohort

Institution	Nonforeign Applicants	Nonforeign Enrolled Students
Private Institutions		
Ivy Universities		
Columbia University	10,066	1,158
Harvard University	15,429	1,511
Princeton University	14,312	1,207
University of Pennsylvania	14,331	2,356
Yale University	12,620	1,364
Liberal Arts Colleges		
Barnard College	2,973	521
Bowdoin College	3,712	436
Macalester College	2,507	437
Middlebury College	3,222	581
Oberlin College	3,985	725
Pomona College	3,583	392
Smith College	3,334	631
Swarthmore College	2,967	354
Wellesley College	3,371	551
Williams College	4,518	513
All Private	**100,930**	**12,737**
Public Universities		
Pennsylvania State University	23,992	4,284
University of California – Los Angeles	25,457	3,695
University Of Illinois –Urbana/ Champaign	16,936	5,998
University of Virginia	13,249	2,810
All Public	79,634	16,787
All Institution	180,564	29,524

Source: Expanded College and Beyond Database.

They looked at the data to answer the question: "Is there an admissions advantage associated with being a poor or a first-generation student that is comparable to the advantage associated with being a minority student, or a legacy student, or a recruited athlete?"

Figure 2: Percent of Applicants, Admitted Students, Enrolled Students, and Graduates who Are Socioeconomically Disadvantaged, All 19 Institutions, 1995 Entering Cohort

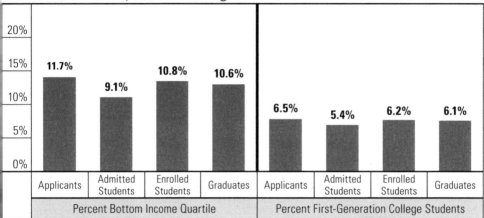

Source: Expanded College and Beyond Database.
Note: Percentages based on nonforeign students who provided income and parental education data on the Student Descriptive Questionnaire.

Tobin shared data (Figure 2) indicating that both low-income and first-generation students are heavily underrepresented in the applicant pools of the 19 surveyed institutions (lowest income quartile students comprise 11 percent; first-generation, just over 6 percent). Only 3 percent of the students at these institutions come from low-income families with no college background, whereas for the national population in 1992, about 19 percent of high school graduates would have fit those criteria.

Another key finding was that these percentages do not change very much when one moves from the applicant pool to the admitted cohort, to those who enroll and, finally, to those who graduate. "This consistent pattern suggests that socioeconomic status does not affect progression through these stages, which leads to a third finding that we believe is stunningly striking. Once disadvantaged students make it into the credible applicant pool for these highly selective institutions—no easy accomplishment—they have essentially the same experiences [in terms of admission, enrollment, and graduation] as their more advantaged peers."

The percentage from the lowest income group is slightly higher at the public institutions, as is the share of first-generation students. But at the four public flagship universities that were part of the research, students from top-income-quartile families earning more than $200,000 outnumber those whose families made less than the national median income of $53,000. Only 4 percent of the students at the flagships were from low-income, first-generation college families. "These parallel profiles between private and public institutions certainly raise questions of mission and public policy."

7

Tobin went on to say that the distribution of SAT scores is more closely correlated with race than income. But average SATs at these institutions are lower with the lowest quartile of income or no parental education (Figure 3).

Figure 3: Probability of Admission of Nonminorities, by Family Income and Parental Education, by SAT Score Range, All 19 Institutions, 1995 Entering Cohort

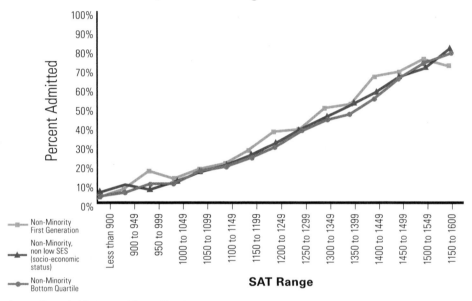

Source: Expanded College and Beyond Database.
Note: Admission rates based on nonforeign applicants who provided income and parental education data on the Student Descriptive Questionnaire.

When examining admissions probabilities for three groups of applicants—nonminority students from the bottom-income quartile, first-generation nonminority students, and all other applicants of higher socioeconomic status who are not members of underrepresented minorities—and when holding SATs constant, they found virtually no difference in the chances of being admitted, at any SAT level, for students from the two low-SES categories and for all nonminority applicants.

"Most of these 19 institutions claim to be need-blind in admissions, and our data suggests that they truly are need-blind. The adjusted admissions advantages enjoyed, however, by four special applicant groups— recruited athletes, minority students, legacies, and early action/early decision candidates—as seen in Figure 4, are far greater than the 4.1 percentage-point boost for first-generation students."

Figure 4: Admission Advantage Associated with Various Characteristics, 13 Institutions, 1995 Entering Cohort

	Admissions Advantage
Income (Relative to Middle Quartiles)	
Bottom Quartile	-1.0
Top Quartile	**-3.1**
Parental Education	
First-Generation College Student	**4.1**
Other Characteristics	
Recruited Athlete	**30.2**
Underrepresented Minority	**27.7**
Legacy	**19.7**
Early Applicant	**19.6**

Source: Expanded College and Beyond Database.
Notes: Numbers in bold are significant to 0.05. Predictions are based on a logistic regression with dependent variable admit, and controls for SAT's, race, income, parental education, recruit status, legacy status, early application, and institutional dummy variables. Penn State, Pomona, Swatrhmore, UCLA, University of Illinois, and Wellesley were excluded due to missing values. Only nonforeign applicants who provided income and parental education data on the Student Descriptive Questionnaire Observations with missing values were excluded.

In other words, an applicant with a typical admissions probability of 40 percent has a 70 percent probability of admission if he or she is a recruited athlete.

In terms of academic performance, Tobin indicated that earlier research reported by William Bowen and Sarah Levin shows that minority students earned lower grades than would have been expected based on their SAT scores, fields of study, and high school grades, and the underperformance of recruited athletes is even more pronounced. Yet students of low socioeconomic background at these 19 institutions do as well as expected: they are not underperforming. "For applicants to these 19 selective institutions who took the SAT and did well, family income and parental education, in and of themselves, had surprisingly little effect on admission probability, matriculation decisions, choice of major, subsequent academic performance, graduation rates, and even on later-life outcomes, such as earnings and civic participation."

Tobin went on to say this does not mean low SES has no effect—but that the effect of low income occurs early on, in the accumulated development of cognitive skills, motivation, expectation, and practical knowledge about the college process. Tobin concedes that the odds of getting into the pool are heavily dependent on one's upbringing. But once students do get into this highly competitive pool, often due to extraordinary efforts of guidance counselors and parents, they perform as well as would be expected.

Tobin asked, "Are the claims of equity really being met through a need-blind admissions approach in a society in which students are stratified in socioeconomic status in their precollege years?" Although the special groups Tobin mentioned earlier enjoy a distinct advantage in the admissions process, students who are from lower socioeconomic groups and are the first to attend college have a virtually identical admissions rate to that of their more privileged counterparts. They receive no advantage in the admissions process, nor are they being penalized for their disadvantaged background.

Tobin then tackled the question of whether, looking ahead, the current set of preferences that exist at these highly selective institutions is the best way to allocate spaces. He believes that minority student preferences serve several basic societal and educational goals, explicitly delineated by the Supreme Court and a multitude of *amicus* briefs filed in the Michigan case: "A diverse student body provides educational benefits to all students. Race matters in America, and that reality needs to be acknowledged in terms of the racial stigmas that profoundly disadvantaged minority students have lived through and continue to live with."

He described legacy admissions as something entirely different, serving to enhance ties between alumni and colleges, which are heavily dependent upon alumni contributions. "But in our view, there is a clear trade-off between the goals of equity—which are not advanced by preferences of this kind—and the goals of excellence, which do depend upon generating resources from alumni and other donors." Tobin cautioned that, to make the excellence argument, colleges should take great care in deciding how much of a break they give children of alumni, and that the numbers not be too large.

Tobin indicated that, in comparison with minority preferences or legacy/development preferences, it is hard to know what institutional goals athletic preferences serve. They serve the interests of the athletic establishment and groups of trustees and alumni who have strong feelings about sports. "Yet recent research reveals all too clearly the ways in which intercollegiate athletics conflict with core academic values at many of the nation's most selective colleges that do not offer athletic scholarships. It seems evident that athletic preferences raise fundamental questions about core commitments, resource allocations, and about what matters most in crafting an incoming class. The fact that recruited athletes underperform academically whether they play or not, also suggests real limitations on continuing these forms of preference."

As for early decision applicants, they also enjoy an advantage in the process. Early decision programs serve prospective students who know where they want to go and will be a great fit at an institution. But the process rewards those who are "fortunate enough" to know applying early can be advantageous. Those who are need-sensitive cannot take advantage of these programs, and minority students are disproportionately represented in the need-sensitive category. "These programs encourage the institutions and students to 'game the system.'" Early decision hurts lower income students and helps college statistics. In sum, Tobin is most comfortable with the preferences given to minority students, which serve larger, societal goals, and least comfortable with the preferences given to athletes, which serve narrower interests.

In conclusion, Tobin reiterated that their data demonstrate that the odds of being in this applicant pool are six times higher for students from high-income families than from poor families, and seven times higher for students from college-educated families than from families with no previous college education. Once these applicants make it into the credible pool, they have essentially the same experiences as other students. Tobin and his coauthors believe "additional steps urgently need to be taken. Poor families simply have a harder time than wealthy families in investing sufficient personal and financial resources to encourage their children's abilities to attend college, to do well, and to graduate." The ultimate solution is to improve the environment for these students. But in the meantime, Tobin believes we need to close the gap.

Tobin shared that some in higher education have suggested that income- or class-based admissions preferences could replace race-conscious preferences. Figure 5 presents a simulation of how a preference for low-income students (if they were given the same advantage as legacy students) could alter selection if the race-sensitive advantages were kept at their current level. The admissions probability for low-income students would increase from 32 percent at present to 47 percent. The admissions probability for all other students falls, but only from 39 percent to 38 percent, the explanation being the relative sizes of the groups in the applicant pool. The percentage of the class composed of low-income students would rise from 11 percent to about 17 percent. The minority share would remain constant at 13 percent and the share of all other students would decline from 79 percent to 74 percent.

Figure 5: A Simulation of the Effects of Income-Sensitive Admission Preferences Based on Legacy Preferences, Retaining Race-Sensitive Preferences, 18 Institutions, 1995 Entering Cohort

	Current Policy	Income-Sensitive Preferences
Admissions Probabilities		
All Bottom Income Quartile	32.1%	46.6%
All Minority	48.3%	48.8%
Nonminority, Non-Bottom Quartile	39.4%	38.2%
Percent of Admitted Students		
All Bottom Income Quartile	9.2%	13.8%
All Minority	15.5%	15.5%
Nonminority, Non-Bottom Quartile	78.6%	74.0%
Percent of Enrolled Students		
All Bottom Income Quartile	10.6%	16.7%
All Minority	13.4%	13.2%
Nonminority, Non-Bottom Quartile	79.4%	73.5%

Source: Expanded College and Beyond Database.
Note: University of Illinois is excluded due to missing legacy data. Numbers may not sum correctly or may differ slightly when they should be the same due to rounding.

Tobin went on to describe a simulation (Figure 6) which shows that, if the institutions opted to preference low-income students at the same rate as legacies, without keeping race-sensitive preferences, "the share of students who are minorities falls by nearly half." Tobin explained that even though African Americans, Hispanics, and Native Americans are disproportionately represented among socioeconomically disadvantaged college applicants, the vast majority of economically disadvantaged candidates are white.

Figure 6: A Simulation of the Effects of Income-Sensitive Admission Preferences Based on Legacy Preferences, Eliminating Race-Sensitive Preferences, 18 Institutions, 1995 Entering Cohort

	Current Policy	Income-Sensitive Preferences
Admissions Probabilities		
All Bottom-Income Quartile	32.1%	43.3%
All Minority	48.3%	26.6%
Nonminority, Non-Bottom Quartile	39.4%	40.5%
Percent of Admitted Students		
All Bottom-Income Quartile	9.2%	13.1%
All Minority	15.5%	8.0%
Nonminority, Non-Bottom Quartile	78.6%	81.3%
Percent of Enrolled Students		
All Bottom-Income Quartile	10.6%	15.7%
All Minority	13.4%	7.1%
Nonminority, Non-Bottom Quartile	79.4%	79.9%

Source: Expanded College and Beyond Database.
Note: University of Illinois is excluded due to missing legacy data. Numbers may not sum correctly or may differ slightly when they should be the same due to rounding.

Tobin stated that there are three kinds of potential costs associated with this hypothetical preference being given to low-income students: "erosion of the academic profile, a decrease in alumni giving, and increased financial aid costs. For various reasons, only the last of these bears out substantially." He and his coauthors estimate that for this group of private liberal arts colleges, with a average of 500 students per class, "grant aid funds would have to increase about $460,000 per class, per year, or just under $2 million for all four classes per year; approximately a 12 percent increase, if current financial aid policies were maintained. For the private universities in our study, with 1,500 students per class, the necessary increase could be expected to be about $1.4 million per class, per year, or between $5 and $6 million for all four classes, which is also approximately a 12 percent increase— not a small amount, but certainly affordable for the 30 or 40 wealthiest colleges and universities in the country."

Tobin concluded, "Equity cannot be achieved through a need-blind admissions approach that was designed a half-century ago when higher education was much more restricted to an elite clientele than it is today. Treating qualified students from low-SES and low-parental education backgrounds exactly the same as all other applicants gives insufficient weight to the accomplishments of students who have bucked the odds by making it into the credible applicant pool. If America's leading colleges and universities are to become genuine agents of social mobility and economic opportunity, complementing affirmative action with a 'thumb on the scale' for academically qualified but socioeconomically disadvantaged students would seem to be an excellent next step and a practical and effective complement to race-based preferences."

The audience then had a chance to respond. Joe Paul Case, dean and director of financial aid, Amherst College, asked, "How do we identify and expand this pool?" Tobin replied, "I want to emphasize that the institutions represented in the survey and others like them are doing what they can to identify these students, based on the availability of information about who is out there. We believe we need to drive down the costs of identifying low-SES students whose performance and scores might not suggest that they would be credible candidates for admission, but who could do college work. At the Mellon Foundation, we want to work with other nonprofit organizations around the country to identify what is estimated to be perhaps as many as 500,000–600,000 students who have the talent but are not being reached. I agree, identifying them is the hardest part."

Lynn Nichelson, director of financial aid, Illinois Wesleyan University, commented, "My concern is that over the last 15 years in this country we have moved from focusing on the societal to the individual benefits of college, and have experienced an erosion of federal and state support of education. How can we get state, federal, and private programs to actively share in the costs of educating these students?" Tobin said, "In our book, we recommend at the state level that the large flagship public institutions be allowed to have their tuition determined by the marketplace, not by the state. Then the state funds can go to the institutions that are carrying the burden of educating the low-SES students. At the federal level, the major changes in higher education funding have been tax credits and reductions, which are of no benefit to the lowest income groups. The federal government would be well served to revisit the Pell grant issue; but this will be a very tough sell."

Bill Hurry, executive director, Rhode Island Higher Education Assistance Authority, stated, "Despite our constant pleas for more money for higher education, I have concluded that the real problems are way, way down the pipeline." Tobin agreed. "We need more money for Head Start through twelfth grade—but we should not take it from higher education. We need to make it possible for those low-SES students who made it to college, to continue and graduate."

Michael Thompson, vice provost for enrollment management and dean of admission and financial aid, University of Southern California, expressed the concern that if colleges and universities across the country permitted themselves to become need-aware in admissions, there would be significantly less opportunity for low-SES students, given budget constraints, at institutions other than the 19 elites in the study. Tobin said, "I am not saying that jettisoning need-blind admission is the solution. I am saying that, if you treat those four highly advantaged groups so advantageously, and the low-income group just like everyone else, that's dead wrong. We need to look at the need-blind policy, which was right at the time it originated, in 1955, when only 40 percent of students were going on to higher education. Now, with over 60 percent going on, and with these special groups getting such an advantage, if we are going to make a difference for the low-SES group, we have to be need-sensitive."

Ann Wright, vice president for enrollment, Rice University, said, "Most of us are not in a position to move money from other budgets into financial aid. What are you doing to make presidents and those at the national level aware of where money could be better spent?" Tobin replied, "One of the good things about the Mellon Foundation is being part of the research and influence. These issues will be generating more attention nationwide."

Betty Cittadine, director, College Bridge, Chicago Public Schools, said, "Urban school systems in this country are struggling with No Child Left Behind; our faculty call it 'No Teacher Left Intact.' What is your feeling about the mandate, and will it provide more students in the pipeline?" Tobin opined, "At best, the results of No Child Left Behind are ambiguous. I don't think it's the solution. It has done some good in some places—but it will not increase the numbers of students prepared for these types of institutions."

Sandy Baum, professor of economics, Skidmore College, and senior policy analyst, the College Board, said, "The implications for financial aid budgets of using need-sensitive preferences—such as increasing the aid budget by 12 percent— are simply not plausible for many institutions. There seems that there would be nothing to be done but raise tuition. What do you say to institutions that really don't have the money to increase their financial aid budget?" Tobin responded, "I would look at how we are spending our money. The amount of money spent on non-core-mission activities is quite high at many institutions. If we were to focus on the core, there might well be money to help put a modest thumb on the scale for low-SES students. Institutions should focus on what their mission says. For example, how much is an institution spending on athletics? I know all of the institutions represented here are making every effort they can. I would like each of you to go back to your institutions and look at your budgets to see if there is any room you can make to admit one, two, or three more students with these types of backgrounds and experiences. In addition to the inspiration it would provide those students, think of the impact it might have on younger siblings or other students from their high schools. I do recognize that it is all about resources, as it always is."

A complete version of Dr. Tobin's remarks may be found in Appendix A.

Eugene Tobin

Eugene Tobin is the program officer in higher education for the Liberal Arts College Program at the Andrew W. Mellon Foundation. His areas of responsibility include efforts aimed at realigning intercollegiate athletic programs more closely with educational values, assisting liberal arts colleges' access to and utilization of instructional technology, and supporting the implementation of a postretirement health care benefits program for college and university faculty. He also advises the foundation on grants relating to faculty development, curricular reform, and postdoctoral fellowships.

Prior to joining the foundation in July 2003, Tobin served as the eighteenth president of Hamilton College (1993–2003), where he was also dean of the faculty (1988–1993) and professor and chair of the department of history (1986–1988). Dr. Tobin earned his B.A. in history from Rutgers University and his M.A. and Ph.D. degrees from Brandeis University.

Prior to his service at Hamilton, Dr. Tobin taught at a number of colleges and universities, including New Jersey City College, Kutztown University, Miami University (Ohio), and Indiana University. His research focuses on twentieth-century American labor and political history from the Progressive Era through the early Cold War. He is the coauthor of *Equity and Excellence in American Higher Education* (with William G. Bowen and Martin A. Kurzweil, University of Virginia Press, April 2005); *Organize or Perish: America's Independent Progressives, 1913–1933* (Greenwood Press, 1986); coauthor with Ann Fagan Ginger of *The National Lawyers Guild: From Roosevelt through Reagan* (Temple University Press, 1988); and coauthor with Michael H. Ebner of *The Age of Urban Reform: New Perspectives on the Progressive Era* (Kennikat Press, 1977). His articles have appeared in *New Jersey History, The American Journal of Economics and Sociology, The Journal of Urban History, The Historian*, and *Labor History.*

The Changing Demography:

Realities, Challenges, and Implications

CHERYL BLANCO, director of policy analysis and research, Western Interstate Commission for Higher Education (WICHE), described the demographic data and research WICHE has recently published in the sixth edition of *Knocking at the College Door*. WICHE has collected 30 years of data; the most recent data was broken down by race/ethnicity and by public school/private school; and, for the first time, projections of graduates by income were included (based on the 2000 census).

Blanco indicated that their projections are based on the assumption of all things being/ remaining equal. It does not take into account No Child Left Behind, new state policy objectives, or reductions in funding that might affect access. Blanco wondered aloud, "What about students who complete their high school graduation requirements but do not pass the high-stakes test to get a diploma: what do we do with them if we cannot consider them graduates?"

In 2008-09, 3.2 million (public and private) high school students are forecast to graduate, more than ever before and an 8 percent increase over the number today. Minority students will be an increasing proportion (43 percent) of this number—a 23 percent increase in five years–and there will be a decline in white students in almost every state.

Regionally, the West and the South will see increases, with the South seeing the largest increase; the Northeast and Midwest will not see much change. Blanco indicated that a lot of the western growth is among very poor populations—these students may not actually graduate. "It is likely we will see states cannibalizing from other states; it will come to getting enough students from out of state to keep your own doors open," Blanco said.

Figure 7: Percent Change in Number of Public and Nonpublic High School Graduates by State, U.S., 2001–2002 (actual) and 2017–2018 (projected)

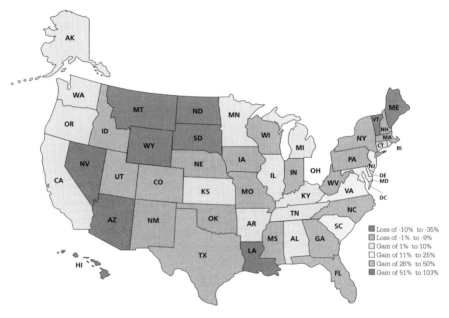

Referring to percentage changes in the projected number of high school graduates between 2001–2002 and 2017–2018, Blanco indicated that some states will see significant percentage losses of 11 to 35 percent (Hawaii, Louisiana, Maine, Montana, North Dakota, South Dakota, Vermont, and Wyoming). Others will see manageable losses of 1 to 10 percent (Iowa, Massachusetts, Missouri, Mississippi, Nebraska, New Hampshire, New Mexico, New York, Oklahoma, Pennsylvania, Wisconsin, and West Virginia). Some states will see manageable growth of 1 to 10 percent (Alaska, Alabama, Arkansas, California, Connecticut, Illinois, Kansas, Kentucky, Michigan, Minnesota, Ohio, Oregon, Rhode Island, Tennessee, and Washington); while others will see considerable growth of 11 to 25 percent (Delaware, Idaho, Maryland, New Jersey, South Carolina, and Virginia). Significant increases (25 to 50 percent) are expected for Colorado, Florida, Georgia, Indiana, North Carolina, Texas, and Utah. Finally, "off the chart" increases will be experienced in Arizona (55 percent) and Nevada (103 percent). Blanco pointed out that the type of growth experienced in Nevada leads to a siphoning of resources from higher education to elementary education, where 34 new schools are being built every year. Arizona is planning to construct a new level in higher education, a middle sector of baccalaureate institutions.

Blanco indicated that the data show a "split dilemma," where half of the states will have a manageable change—plus or minus—to accommodate, while a fifth will see high growth that will be more difficult to manage; a small number will see declines of up to 25 percent. "This is a *state* problem, not a federal one—the onus will be on the states to deal with it."

She also pointed out that a surge in Hispanic and Asian/Pacific Islander student enrollment is driving the trend toward minority majorities in a number of states, particularly in the West.

Figure 8: The New Minority Majority

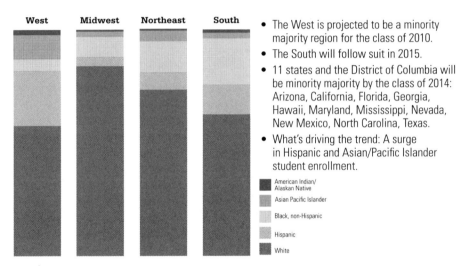

- The West is projected to be a minority majority region for the class of 2010.
- The South will follow suit in 2015.
- 11 states and the District of Columbia will be minority majority by the class of 2014: Arizona, California, Florida, Georgia, Hawaii, Maryland, Mississippi, Nevada, New Mexico, North Carolina, Texas.
- What's driving the trend: A surge in Hispanic and Asian/Pacific Islander student enrollment.

Blanco went on to describe some of the WICHE income data. She shared that about half of the new high school graduates in 2017–2018 (half of 3.2 million students) will be from families earning less than $50,000 annually. "There will be a dramatic increase in the need for state and institutional aid." Fully one-fifth of the high school graduates in the South, and about 17 percent of those in the West, will come from families making less than $20,000 a year. Blanco warned, "This information is projected from 1999 income data reported in the 2000 census; incomes now are not as high as they were then, so I fear these numbers understate the problem. And the regional data dilute the individual state data; for example, 27 percent of New Mexico graduates will be from low-income families."

Figure 9: Distribution of Public High School Graduates by Family Income, U.S., 2006–2007 (projected)

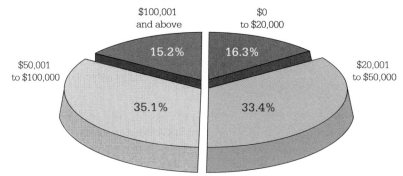

Building on the income data, Blanco went on to describe how low-income students progress differently through K–12 schools. For example, in a theoretical progression of 1,000 hypothetical students in the South, 655 from the lowest income group will graduate, as compared with 810 from the highest income group. Blanco went on to very quickly review data from selected states. In conclusion, Blanco urged the participants to check out the state-by-date data from *Knocking at the College Door* at their Web site, www.wiche.edu.

Don Heller, associate professor and senior research associate, Center for the Study of Higher Education, The Pennsylvania State University, said that the percentage increase in high school graduates by 2008–2009 translates to 1.1 million more undergraduate students in our higher education institutions than this year, based on current participation rates. He predicts many of them will be going to community colleges and proprietary schools.

Heller echoed Blanco's concern that a proportionately greater number of these future high school graduates will need financial assistance; indeed, he expects half of them will be Pell-eligible. But Heller indicated the money needed by these students "will not be coming from the federal government in any amount proportionate to the level of demand and eligibility." There will be increased borrowing, but he reminded the group that students at the lowest income levels have traditionally been reluctant to borrow money to pay for education. Heller predicts tuition will continue to rise, the lowest income students will continue not to want to borrow money, and the demand for aid will have to be met by the states and the institutions. While expressing skepticism that No Child Left Behind will indeed prepare more students for higher education, to the extent that more students *may* graduate and be prepared to go to college, they will be disproportionately minority students and disproportionately lower income students, further increasing the demand for financial assistance.

Heller indicated that selective and highly selective colleges and universities will not be the institutions accommodating these new students. "Even if the 19 institutions in Dr. Tobin's study doubled the proportion of low-income students they took in, that would absorb only 3,000 students nationwide. If you expand that to the entire group of most selective or highly selective institutions, those institutions are not going to absorb this large number of students: the number of seats at those institutions is largely fixed. Public institutions and, to be honest, especially the less selective ones, will have to take them in—and they generally have the fewest resources."

Finally, he cautioned that these data do not deal with the population of adult students, which will grow as well. Heller expects some of the high school graduates in the projections, if unable to go immediately to college, will attend college later as adults. "We need to think outside the box—there is no structure in place to deal with that scenario."

The audience then had a chance to respond. Peter Osgood, director of admissions, Harvey Mudd College, asked Blanco, "Is there any more information about the move to or from rural areas in terms of population shift?" She replied, "As the population declines, it declines most severely in the rural areas. And high-quality educational services simply cannot be delivered in the smallest systems, further disadvantaging those students and keeping them from being ready for college. People go where the jobs are."

Bill Hurry asked, "What about distance learning and alternate delivery systems, using the Internet? Some congressional leaders involved in reauthorization are pushing that option." Blanco responded, "The pressure is going to be out there for institutions to do more partnering, sharing curricula and programs, and the federal government will help fund such efforts." She shared that Carol Twigg of the Center for Academic Transformation has been able to demonstrate that institutions can increase efficiencies by delivering introductory math and English classes by computer. "We need to do research on how this type of learning affects different levels of kids. Students are often not ready at the high school level to take highly challenging levels of course work online." Heller added, "There will be some interesting things coming out in terms of technology—but from what I have seen, the cost savings will be marginal. Technology is not the silver bullet that will get tuition rates down to or below the rate of inflation."

Henry Ingle, associate vice president, Office of Technology, Planning, and Distance Learning, University of Texas at El Paso, asked, "Is there any vision regarding in-state and out-of-state tuition? Also, what about the decline in Ph.D.'s as we aim to educate more students?" Blanco responded that in Ohio they have eliminated the difference in tuition for in-state and out-of-state students. "State legislators grapple with how to defend similar costs for both groups. And colleges like to maximize their revenues by bringing in more out-of-state students. It is a very complex issue; I do not see a lot of states in my region heading in this direction." As for the graying faculty, Blanco sees that as "a major, major issue. There have been so many other problems to deal with, it has been hard to raise the level of interest in this problem. The lack of faculty salary growth and the kidnapping of faculty have added to the severity of the problem."

Roger Koester, director of financial aid, Colorado School of Mines, commented about Colorado's College Opportunity Fund Stipend (voucher system) established by the legislature, which he sees as "an insidious plot to be able to cut higher education funding by over a third." Tuitions are rising rapidly in the state, and the vouchers will deliver only two-thirds of the funding that state schools now receive from the state. Given that the population is predicted to increase significantly, Koester sees Colorado as one of the states most at risk in terms of higher education funding and population growth, and the economic situation is not improving.

Cathy Thomas, associate dean of enrollment services, University of Southern California, said, "I am concerned about getting these new students through to college graduation, and the financial resources institutions will have to expend once the students are on campus. We cannot offer false promise to these students. It is a real policy issue." Heller agreed, "These additional students will need ongoing, campus-based help to persist and graduate, not just financial aid." Blanco added, "New Mexico has taken an unprecedented step to design legislation that would provide performance-based incentives to institutions that increase the number of Pell students who persist to the second year, who transfer to four-year institutions, and who graduate. This is a very poor state, but they are putting their money where they feel their high priority is."

Classism:

The Greatest Obstacle to Connecting to Higher Education

Essayist and social critic Peter Sacks shared a number of perspectives surrounding the issue of class and its relationship to higher education. These insights will be featured in his forthcoming book and, therefore, Mr. Sacks and his editors have requested that only a synopsis of his remarks be included in the proceedings.

- While the United States nominally has a free and open educational system, real inequities exist. When inequality is discussed, the focus is on gender and race. Most American citizens think that they are middle class: the real class divisions that exist are not discussed. Sacks believes class is the dominant organizing principle of higher education, but exists under the cultural radar screen.

- Only 6 percent of students from families earning $35,000 or less earn a bachelor's degree by their twenty-fourth birthday. In the top income group, 50 percent of students have earned a bachelor's degree by age 24. Seventy of 100 students in the 146 top-ranked colleges are from the top quarter in income; 3 of 100 in these same schools come from the bottom-income quartile.

- Looking at the 50 most selective institutions, one's odds of attendance are evenly spread in terms of race. But in terms of income, there is a dramatic imbalance. One's father's income and occupation are more powerful influences on whether or not one is admitted.

- Standardized tests have assumed a place their creators could not have predicted. They are part of the culture of gatekeeping. Rank ordering applicants by test scores is a major problem.

- Colleges and universities promote and profit by concerns about status. Americans spend money and effort on a small group of elite colleges. Only a tiny group of students can play the elite college game. It is a game about social status, where it is assumed there are no good choices below the intellectually elite schools.

- In the Supreme Court ruling regarding affirmative action, the majority opinion supported the use of affirmative action because college provides pathways to leadership. The most selective institutions provide the most efficient paths to leadership. If class does determine who gets to attend those institutions, we are creating a self-perpetuating inequality system.

- State and federal governments have created a policy that is at war with the lower classes, replacing grants with loans. Pell grants used to cover 85 percent of the average tuition but now cover less than half. Increases in the awarding of merit aid take from the politically weak and give to the politically powerful middle and upper income groups. In sum, there are dangerous levels of inequality in the higher education system, and there is a massive shift away from opening access to the poor.

23

- Appropriate responses for higher education include the need to pay more than lip service to creating access. The proportion of colleges and universities looking at low-income students is half the number that are focusing on affirmative action. Affirmative action is the right thing to do, but it only goes so far. It has not helped the lowest income African American students attend elite institutions. Removing one's institution from the rankings game would also help. The ranking system lacks a focus on what students really need. Colleges and universities should lead the way to bring social class to the foreground and to explore the collective problems of class stratification.

Connecting the First-Year Experience to Improved Retention

RANDY SWING, codirector and senior scholar, Policy Center on the First Year of College, echoed a concern Linda Dagradi of the colloquium planning committee had shared with him earlier, "Access is an empty promise if it is not followed by student success in terms of graduation and learning." He told the audience about his experiences as a young, rural North Carolinian going to community college after high school. In doing so, he encouraged the participants to share *their* stories with students, believing that many in the admissions and aid professions bring passion to what they do because of the obstacles they overcame to achieve higher education opportunities, and students could be inspired by their stories.

Swing listed a number of factors determined by the Educational Testing Service to heighten the chances of a student's dropping out of college. Students who experience two to four of these factors are at moderate risk of attrition; those with five or more are at high risk:

- academically underprepared
- single parent
- financially independent
- caring for children at home
- working more than 30 hours per week
- first-generation college student
- being a part-time student
- college cost is a significant issue

Swing indicated the four factors that were an issue for him. He added that he is considered a drop-out from Davidson County Community College—given how statistics are kept—even though he completed bachelor's, master's, and doctoral degrees elsewhere and even though he views the community college as a place that shaped his life and prepared him to continue his education (he opted not to take a course required for an associate degree because it was not required by the college to which he transferred as a junior). "Do you view this as a failure of the community college system? I certainly don't."

He went on to debunk some popular myths about student retention, in particular one that says that students are most likely to drop out during the first six weeks. This myth was popularized by Lee Noel and Randi Levitz in a 1989 book chapter referring to an unpublished research report (1981) that focused on one institution, St. Cloud State University in Minnesota. "The actual quotation is 'Of the students who left during the first term, 50 percent left during the first six weeks.' Somehow this has been translated into the belief that students who drop out of college make the decision in the first six weeks. I've been on campuses where the first-year seminar lasts exactly six weeks—after that, the students are on their own, because they are considered saved.

"That leads me to the problem we have with correlation and causation. I want to be sure you understand that what we read about retention is not always so." For example, some researchers found that institutions that had spent more money on library books had higher retention rates. "That makes sense: colleges with higher retention rates can afford to spend more money on library books. But they determined, using partial regression analysis of this fact, that a one percent gain in retention could be had for every additional $44 spent on library books."

Another example of correlation/causation confusion stems from the fact that students who belong to clubs and organizations are retained at higher levels than students who do not. An institution I know decided to take this fact and simply require all students to belong to a club or organization."

Next, Swing challenged the group to rethink their "knowledge" of high-risk students (those who have five or more of the characteristics he outlined earlier) by taking the following true-false quiz.

What do you know about high-risk students?

(True or False)
High-risk students are more likely to...

- come to class unprepared
- ask questions in class
- prepare 2+ drafts of papers/assignments
- report "working harder than they thought they could to meet instructor's expectations"
- devote more time to class preparation (even though they also work more hours per week)

The correct responses come from "Engaging Community Colleges: A First Look" by Kay McClenney. High-risk students were 11 percent less likely to come to class unprepared than other students, more likely to ask questions in class, more likely to prepare multiple drafts of assignments, and more likely to report working harder than they thought they could; and they experienced no difference in the amount of time they devote to class preparation. "High-risk students have to exert more effort to succeed, and many of them work harder because they know they are at risk. When high-risk students drop out, it is most likely when out-of-class conditions overwhelm them, when life gets in the way."

Swing outlined a current debate in retention studies as to what matters most: Is it who students are, or what institutions do? "Obviously, it is both." Swing said Alexander Astin's research indicates 86 percent of the variance in outcomes can be explained by variance in inputs. The National Survey of Student Engagement (NSSE) measures what students do, how they spend their time, where they put their energies, and the like. Swing shared these key NSSE findings:

• What matters most is what students do, not who they are.

• A key factor is the quality of the effort students expend.

• Educationally effective institutions channel student energy toward the right activities.

"So what matters most is what students do—*but* it's what institutions do that helps determine what students do."

Swing then focused on understanding retention. "The data we use are really not very good. We do not have a national tracking system, so we rely on institutional self-reports, or commissioned studies by the National Center for Educational Statistics (NCES), or U.S. census-based studies, using data not designed for such use. The idea that one institution educates a student is not the reality; a Lumina Foundation research report in 2003 (by Ewell, Schild, and Paulson) indicates that "more than half of students attend more than one institution in their pursuit of a bachelor's degree."

Swing shared elements of a descriptive summary of NCES data, showing what was happening with college students six years after their initial matriculation at a four-year institution.

Figure 10: After 6 Years—Initial Institution (4-Yr)

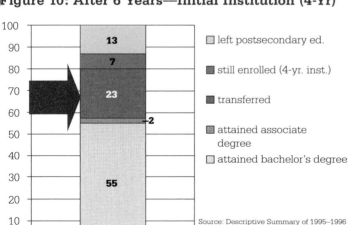

Source: Descriptive Summary of 1995–1996
Beginning Postsecondary Students:
Six Years Later (NCES 2003- 151)

Of 100 who started, 55 percent had attained a bachelor's degree from the institution they started at; 2 percent had attained an associate degree; 23 percent had transferred to another campus; 7 percent were still enrolled at the original institution but had not earned a degree; and 13 percent were no longer in higher education and did not have a degree. "Does that seem like a bad track record to you? Yet, what we usually see in the media is that 55 percent of students have a bachelor's degree after six years, because we only see institution-specific records. Obviously, the 13 students who did not make it concern me; higher education changed my life. But 80 percent are making progress toward or have a degree." Referring to the 23 that left the initial institution, three earned an associate degree elsewhere; seven got a bachelor's degree elsewhere; five are still enrolled in four-year programs elsewhere; two are enrolled at two-year institutions; and six had actually left postsecondary education. "We have focused on the institutional completion rate, not the *student* completion rate."

Swing then wondered if, after three decades of focus on retention and the implementation of retention programs, we have really made a difference. He said there had actually been an increase in the persistence rate between 1990 and 1995.

Graduation or Persistence over 5 years (4-year institutions)

	Degree Completed	Still Enrolled	No Degree, Not Enrolled
1989-90	60.3%	15.2%	24.4%
1995-96	59.3%	20.4%*	20.4%*

*Significant at .05

Graduation or Persistence	75.5%	79.7%
	1989-90	1990-95

Source: NCES 2005-156

28

He also cautioned that graduation rates vary widely, from less than 10 percent at some institutions to almost 100 percent at others. "The average masks the differences." Swing shared data from the Education Trust that reveals the variations that can occur. Of the 42 universities that are similar to the University of Northern Iowa (i.e., educate the same types of students), which has a graduation rate of 67 percent, the median graduation rate of the peer institutions is 48 percent, but nine have rates below 40 percent.

Focusing next on successful retention programs, Swing described efforts at Berea College, the Community College of Denver, and the University of Mississippi. A 1996 study indicated that Berea's retention rate was strong, but not as strong for African American students. Berea developed a series of initiatives both inside and outside the classroom, resulting in a 10 percent increase in overall retention and a major increase in African American retention.

Berea College—Retention Success
(Work college serving low-income students. The South's first interracial and coeductional college.)

Year/1-2 retention

	1996	1998	2001
African Americans less than $25,000	64%	90%	91%
All students less than $25,000	63%	78%	82%

"The centerpiece of their program was faculty adviser training. They decided that the people who were closest to the students had to understand low-income students.

"The Community College of Denver enrolls the types of students who should not graduate in large numbers." They have large numbers of low-income, part-time, first-generation, physically handicapped, minority, and adult students. "In spite of that, by the late 1990s there were no significant differences in student success indicators—persistence, graduation, transfer rates—based on race, ethnicity, age, or gender. By 1995, those who started at the Community College of Denver in a developmental studies class were as likely to graduate as those who did not; and, by 1999, enrollment in a developmental studies course was a *predictor* of success." The institution did this through a case management system, "where they decided that they would not allow life to get in the way of their students graduating. They took instructional dollars to hire case management workers to make sure that low-income students and those in remedial courses know about food stamps, have transportation, have a job, have babysitting backups: they have access to the kinds of services that allow them to come to class and to succeed."

He continued, "We know first-semester and first-year grade point averages are correlated with retention and earning a bachelor's degree. Students who go to class have higher grade point averages. Wouldn't it be helpful if we showed students the path to success? Yet only 7 percent of institutions have a special policy on class attendance for first-year students." Swing described a program at the University of Mississippi that focused on first-year students who had been absent from class twice in the first eight weeks. Faculty reported to the administration about the absences; half got follow-up and half did not. The follow-up consisted of a graduate student calling the absent student on the phone to say he/she had been reported as missing classes and asked if there was anything the university could do. Most students said no. The graduate student told them that going to class matters, and most of the students just thanked them. "Of the students who were contacted, 87 percent had a C or better GPA by the end of the term, compared to 55 percent of those who did not get the intervention." The next year, they contacted everybody who missed two classes in the first eight weeks, with calls made by residence hall advisers; the results dropped somewhat—yet a full 70 percent ended the term with a C or better average.

In these and any other retention efforts, Swing emphasized the importance of "getting buy-in from the faculty; the student affairs folks and the enrollment management folks already get it. We need to work harder at helping faculty understand how what we are focused on is part of what they really want; we need to help them see what the institution is doing to help the students in their class learn and succeed." Swing also said that institutions have to disaggregate their data, so that the right solutions are delivered to the right students.

Finally, Swing said that retention and the first college year are a web of interconnected events. In "Foundations of Excellence in the First College Year," the Policy Center on the First Year of College, with the American Association of State Colleges and Universities (AASCU) and the Council of Independent Colleges (CIC), has developed "dimensions of excellence," broad statements about what matters in the first year of college. The report shows institutions how to evaluate how well they are achieving these standards, using an inclusive task force. Swing emphasized that it is important to determine what an institution is doing well and what it is not doing well, to identify potential solutions, and to determine how to implement those solutions. "Most colleges have simply gathered a basketful of interventions and dumped them into the first-year experience." He urged participants to review the "Foundations of Excellence in the First College Year" report, which can be found at www.fyfoundations.org. Swing indicated that this project has worked very well and will go nationwide at some point.

The audience then had a chance to respond. Joellen Silberman, dean of enrollment, Kalamazoo College, said, "Getting faculty involvement is difficult. The ones who show up for training are the ones who do not need training. How can we get them involved?" Swing replied, "You have to show them that it matters and leads to some good. The task force I described had to identify everything that was being done for the first-year experience. The faculty got to see how broad an effort it was, and they found the complexity fascinating."

Julia Benz, director of student financial services, Rice University, asked about the 23 percent of students who had transferred in the study Swing presented. "What do you think of the individual student data that the federal government collects?" Swing responded that the federal data are not too far off these days. "But the devil is in the details; the definitions won't be right to begin with. Shouldn't we ourselves be gathering comprehensive data? It can actually change how the government sees us. We may have taken privacy too far. I am in favor of more data—we can show that we are doing it right."

Mayten Sanchez, director of admissions, Bloomfield College, asked, "How do you invest in developmental classes on a campus and avoid the stigma?" Swing responded, "One key indicator of success in our task forces was the common theme of involvement of the chief academic officer. It is rare for a grassroots effort to carry it to excellence. Programs need grassroots efforts getting support from the vice president for academic affairs. Also, the institutions in the book had been working 10 years or more in developing a first-year program; it doesn't happen overnight. It is tough, since academic affairs officers are often not in their position very long, and they want to become presidents, so it is hard to get them to take a lead in these types of efforts."

Education Pays:

The Benefits of Higher Education for Individuals and Society

SANDY BAUM, professor of economics, Skidmore College, and senior policy analyst, the College Board, shared insights from the data reported in the College Board publication of the same title. According to Baum, "the goal of the publication is to initiate talk about the cost of not going to college, rather than simply about college costs."

Baum began with the more obvious benefits. "Unfortunately, the focus in society today is on the private benefits of a college education, and especially the private financial benefits. Yet if we look at unemployment, while almost everyone would agree it is a private loss, it is a societal loss as well, in terms of decreased productivity." Baum outlined how a college education relates to median earnings (an individual benefit) as well as tax payments (a public benefit).

**Figure 11: Median Earnings and
Tax Payments by Level of Education, 2003**

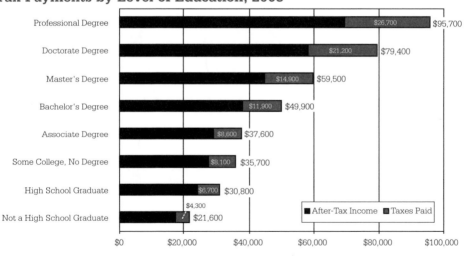

The earnings premium for increased levels of education translates into an increase in taxes paid to public treasuries. For example, in 2003, the median earnings of someone with a professional degree were $95,700, with total estimated taxes of $26,700; for someone with less than a high school diploma, the earnings median was $21,600, with total estimated taxes of $4,300. Baum pointed out, "The difference in earnings between a bachelor's degree holder and one with a professional degree is almost $46,000, but the tax increase is over $14,000—almost a third of those extra earnings are going to the public: they are a shared benefit. So talking only about earnings really exaggerates the extent to which it is the student who is getting the dollar benefit from that higher level of education.

"This pecuniary benefit to society is an argument that can be made for increasing access to college, beyond the argument of basic fairness.

"On the other side, public expenditures are reduced as a result of the fact that more educated people are more financially secure." Data indicates that increased education results in a savings on social programs; educated people make fewer demands in general on such programs. Baum shared the following data from "a very careful and complex statistical study by the Rand Corporation."

Figure 12: Annual Savings on Social Programs from Increased Education: Savings for 30-Year-Old Men and Women Relative to High School Dropouts, 2003 Dollars

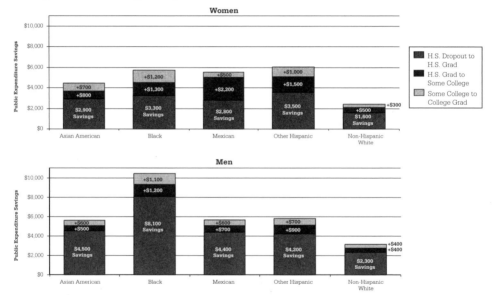

"For example, a typical 30-year-old, non-Hispanic white woman who graduates from high school instead of dropping out results in an annual savings of $1,600 on public programs such as Medicaid, Medicare, or food stamps. If she also had some college education, it would result in another $500 in public savings, and if she graduated from college, that would save another $300 for the public. For other demographic groups, the savings are even greater; but in all cases, the public spends less on people who have gone to college than on those who have not. There is a really good return to the public on the investment. A dollar invested in education will pay us back more than a dollar; it will actually save us money."

Baum went on to describe education level relative to lifetime earnings. "This is one way to encourage students to go on to higher education." The following chart shows lifetime earnings relative to those of a high school graduate (indicated as 1.00 on the chart). The

average college graduate will earn 73 percent more over a lifetime than a high school
graduate; those with a professional or doctoral degree will earn three times as much.

**Figure 13: Expected Lifetime Earnings Relative to High School
Graduates, by Education Level**

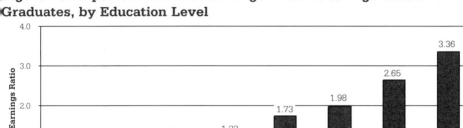

"This is census-based data. I know many of you have heard the figure that a person with
a college degree will earn a million dollars more than a high school graduate. But what the
Census Bureau does is to look at the difference in median earnings of people at every age and
add up the dollar amounts over the course of a 40-year work period. The problem is that if you
make $50,000 in 20 years as opposed to right now, the Census Bureau methodology exaggerates
the return. We looked at the amounts and discounted them by an annual rate of 5 percent
to account for the reality that dollars received in the future are not worth as much as those
received today. If you do that, you come up with an earnings premium for a college graduate of
about $400,000 to $500,000 over a lifetime. A lot of this benefit comes later in life."

Figure 14: Estimated Cumulative Net Earnings of College Costs

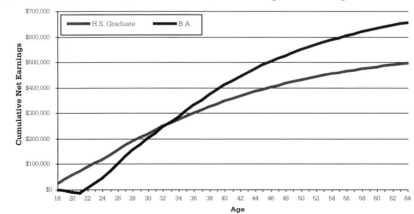

Baum described how the average cumulative earnings curve works, based on the fact that education costs money. In year one, an 18-year-old chooses to go to work (earning money) or to go to college (spending money). The chart uses the average public college tuition and fees for students entering in 2003 ($5,000). By age 33, the earnings graphs cross over, with the college-educated person earning more, if he or she attended public college, than the high school graduate. Baum told the group that, for those who attended a private college, it takes until age 40 on average to cross over. If they had not accounted for the 5 percent annual discount, the crossovers would have occurred at age 30 and 33, respectively. "So, at a relatively young age, you are better off financially with a college degree than without. And this is true for every demographic group."

Baum also indicated that while there is a payoff to education for every racial group and for both genders, there are still "disturbing differences" in earnings, especially among racial groups.

Figure 15: Median Earnings by Race/Ethnicity and Education Level, 2003: Ages 25–34

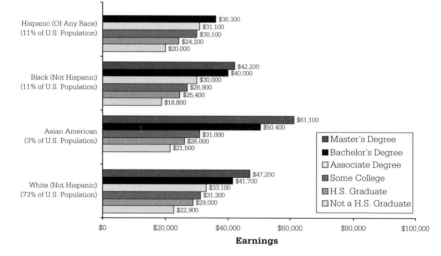

"It is important to look at these percentiles and share them with students because students tend to think that they will be average or above in terms of earnings: they need to see the whole range of incomes. Many students get into debt, thinking that they will ultimately earn more than they do."

Figure 16: Median Earnings of Males and Females
Ages 25–34 by Education Level, 1971–2002 (Constant 2002 Dollars)

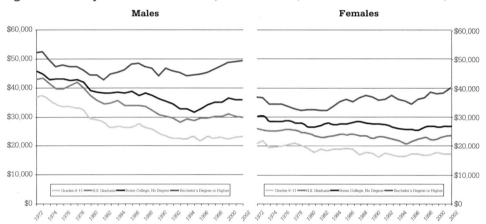

Baum explained, "While the earnings gap between high school and college graduates has grown, it is more due to the fact that incomes have declined for high school graduates, than that college education has increased earnings. College-educated men now have lower incomes in constant dollars than previously, but the decline in earnings is less dramatic for this group than for the high school graduates."

Baum's research also showed less tangible but important outcomes of postsecondary education (in looking at these different experiences, Baum cautioned that "we need to sort out the difference between correlation and causation").

Figure 17: Smoking by Education Level, 1940–2000

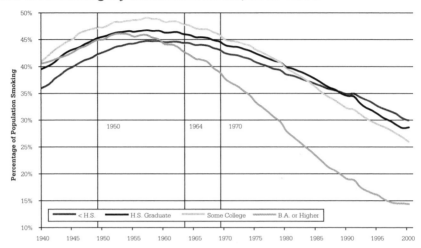

Smoking declines as the education level increases. The information about reduced smoking comes from a complicated statistical study, showing what has happened to smoking behaviors over time. As information about the dangers of smoking became generally known, college graduates responded differently than others. "Everyone smokes less than they did in 1950, but the decline was much steeper for college graduates. This is not just about smoking, or about health and the health care costs to the wider society, it's also about responses to information and how people take responsibility. It is more interesting than just looking at a comparison of smoking rates."

Baum went on to describe research that indicates that preschool children's cognitive skills are enhanced by having mothers with postsecondary education. "Obviously, it is not the case that if you go to college you are automatically going to produce smarter children. This is just part of the socioeconomic environment that Dr. Tobin described, but a slew of indicators show that a child is definitely better off if his or her mother went to college." Similar results were found in terms of children's family activities and kindergartners' learning attitudes. "The children of college graduates are simply more prepared to learn by the time they reach kindergarten."

In reference to other benefits of higher education for society as a whole, Baum shared that higher levels of education are associated with higher levels of participation in volunteer activities. Also, in every age group, adults with higher levels of education are more likely to vote than those who have less education. While voting rates have declined overall since the late 1960s, they have declined more precipitously for those with lower levels of education: differences in voting rates by education level have increased over time. Finally, Baum pointed out that college graduates are more likely than other adults to donate blood.

"This type of information tells us something about attitudes. If we control for income, gender, and ethnicity, we find these attitudes and intangible benefits to society hold true for college graduates. The benefits to society of educated people are financial and civic. Society is better off if people are productive and share in the community effort."

Then Baum moved her focus toward the *distribution* of the benefits that accrue to those with higher levels of education and the communities they live in. "Of course, the biggest differences in socioeconomic levels are attributable to whether one graduates from high school or not. And one can make an argument that not everyone should graduate from college. But let's look at what is happening in terms of opportunity for those with the ability and qualifications to attend college."

Figure 18: Postsecondary Enrollment Rates of 1992 High School Graduates by Family Income and Math Test Scores

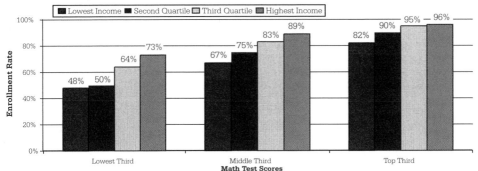

Postsecondary Enrollment Rates of 1992 High School Graduates by Family Income and Parent Education Level

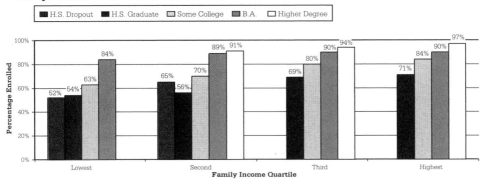

In looking at the data regarding family income and math test scores, 82 percent who were prepared went to college from the lowest income group. "Income differences tend to have a smaller impact on college enrollment rates of high school graduates with high test scores than on those with lower test scores. Differences in academic achievement affect the behavior of low-income students much more than they affect the behavior of high-income students." And, even if a student comes from a low-income family, he or she is more likely to go to college if the parents went to college. If a student comes from a high-income family, he or she is less likely to go to college if the parents did not attend.

Figure 19: Income Distribution of Full-Time, First-Year Students Within Sectors, 1999–2000

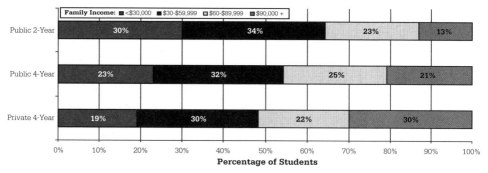

Baum said, "This shows the stratification by income at different types of institutions. The lowest income students are overrepresented in public two-year colleges and underrepresented in private four-year colleges. In the private four-year sector, 30 percent of students are from the highest income level, and only 19 percent are from families with incomes below $30,000.

"This is essentially the same data, wrapped differently, showing the gaps that remain in access. Focusing on first-year students makes these gaps more obvious than other data you may have seen. We need to communicate to the public why education matters and why these gaps matter."

The audience then had a chance to respond. Rebecca Dixon, associate provost of university enrollment, Northwestern University, referred to the chart about the median earnings of males and females. "Is this why more women than men are going to college from high school? Is it because the gain is greater?" Baum replied, "I have looked into the difference, and the studies say that the difference in return does not seem to be the explanation. I think we have to look at the opportunities for 18-year-old male high school graduates versus those for females."

Michael Scott, director of scholarships and financial aid, Texas Christian University, commented, "Looking at the income differentials between high school and college education: What if we manage to get all these kids into college? What does that do to supply and demand?" Baum conceded, "If everyone went to college, the payoff would diminish. But, if we look at what has happened over recent decades, as the percentage of college graduates has grown, the demand for those graduates has increased more rapidly than the supply. Not everyone should go to college—but those who can benefit from a college education, should."

Henry Ingle asked, "How do we compare with other countries in the percentage of college graduates? And how do international students who come here for a degree fare when they go back to their home countries?" Baum replied, "There are some data from OECD (Organization for Economic Cooperation and Development) at the end of *Education Pays*, so you may want to look there. There has been a greater improvement in participation rates in many other countries than here. In terms of educational attainment, we actually do better. It is very, very difficult to make these comparisons, as the educations systems are different. As for what happens to people educated here and the political advantages to the U.S. when they return to their home countries, the decline in international students attending college in the U.S. is an issue to be concerned about."

Doug Christiansen, assistant vice president for enrollment management and dean of admissions, Purdue University, asked about the distribution of *Education Pays*. "What is the College Board's approach to set up and change the debate from private benefits to public benefits of higher education?" Baum said, "The book is going to all college presidents and, at some level, to state legislators, and we are also looking at issuing some briefs from it. If you would like to see this information in some specific format, or distributed to particular groups of people, please give your feedback to the College Board."

All illustrations are reproduced from the College Board publication *Education Pays: The Benefits of Higher Education for Individuals and Society* © 2004.

State Models for Increasing Access to Higher Education

GRETCHEN BATAILLE, senior vice president of academic affairs, University of North Carolina, at Chapel Hill, led off. "Yesterday we looked at lots of national data regarding access and equity. Our goal now is to drill down into the efforts three states are making to promote these ideals."

She began by providing a context for the change in approach toward higher education in North Carolina. In terms of economics, the state, which has historically had a manufacturing and agricultural base, will continue to lose such jobs. "These losses will make a huge difference in the expectations we have for education of our students." The future is in biotechnology, pharmaceuticals, and other technology fields.

As for demographic changes, the state will experience a dramatic increase in the number of high school graduates; and by 2014, there will be more Hispanic than African American high school graduates. "That is a huge cultural shift for the state, and it changes the way people think about education. We are a state with five historically black universities and one Native American university. Some people are asking when we will start our Hispanic university. Because of the traditional manufacturing base, many high school students have not aspired to or been encouraged to attend college. If you look at 100 students in the ninth grade, only 18 of them will graduate from college within six years of entrance. This is not very encouraging for a state that is moving toward a knowledge-based economy."

National trends are also having an impact. The share of family income required to pay for tuition at public colleges has gone up. Bataille also mentioned Pell grants, which are declining. "When we look at these figures, we realize how important it is to figure out where financial aid is going to come from."

In the face of these issues, the College Foundation of North Carolina (CFNC) was formed, "creating one place where students can plan, apply, and pay for college. Our primary goal is access. We are going to increase the college-going rate in North Carolina, paying particular attention to first-generation college students. Our first-generation students face two obstacles: they don't really believe they can go to college, and they don't really believe they can afford to go to college."

Among the foundation's achievements are:

- a standardized high school transcript statewide
- a common grading and weighting system
- expanded and increased minimum course requirements that are now the same throughout the 16-campus UNC system

- a comprehensive articulation agreement
- UNC and CC need-based aid programs
- a $3.1 billion bond program for building and renovations on campuses, to accommodate an increase in students

Bataille then described how three entities comprise the College Foundation of North Carolina: the state's loan originator, a state-funded K–16 partnership (Pathways), and the state guarantor of scholarships. "CFNC is a virtual entity: it doesn't really exist. We offer three services: technology and Internet services, a resource center, and GEAR UP North Carolina, with now almost $9 million in grant funds."

College Foundation of North Carolina	CFNC Access Services	
Technology and Internet Services	**Resource Center**	**GEAR UP North Carolina**
www.CFNC.org	1.866.866.CFNC	Low-income (FRL) school students
Career Center		$8.8 million
Student Planner	Toll-free Telephone Hotline for Career & College Planning	
College Fair		6-year grant from Dept of Education
Online Applications and HS Transcripts	Email from CFNC.org	
	Publications	20 NC counties
Paying for College	Training	6,000+ students

Students can apply to any North Carolina college through CFNC.org, and redirect their applications to other campuses if they do not get into UNC-Chapel Hill. If a student makes an attempt to apply to a college, they will hear from at least the local community college. The information is available in English and Spanish.

They have marketed CFNC though a campaign to raise awareness of the program, using TV, radio, billboards, public service announcements, CD's, and collateral materials.

As a result of their efforts, the Web site gets 5,300 visits a day; they have 700,000 student accounts; and 200,000 applications as of November 2004 had been submitted online.

Figure 20: CFNC.org Account Holders: Grade-Level Yearly Comparison

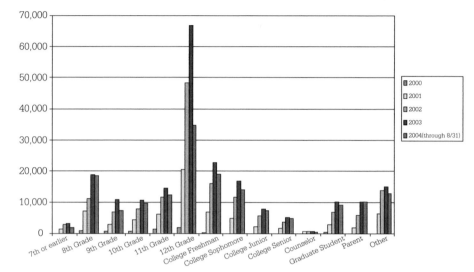

The majority of account holders are twelfth-graders, but the goal is to increase the number of eighth-graders who access the site, and that is happening.

In conclusion, Bataille shared several CFNC television ads that have aired in North Carolina, which were met with great enthusiasm and appreciation by the audience.

William H. Hurry, Jr., executive director, Rhode Island Higher Education Assistance Authority, spoke next. He indicated that efforts to increase access to higher education in Rhode Island were not as systematized as in North Carolina. "We in Rhode Island, like many of you, struggle to develop and fund initiatives to cope with—not necessarily to solve—the systemic problems that contribute to a lack of access. Although our state is small, it is very decentralized; we like to work in smaller groups and are more comfortable with local control. This makes it hard to push big K–12 projects forward."

Hurry shared demographic and economic information for his state, highlights of which are:

- By 2025, the tradition college age population will decline 2.2 percent
- Ethnic background of the current population: 85 percent white; 8.7 percent Hispanic/Latino; 4.5 percent African American; 2.3 percent Asian
- Average annual earnings for families of low to middle income college students: $21,000
- Percentage of families with children under 18 living in poverty: 16.1 percent
- Rhode Island is in the top 10 states for the education level of its workforce

- Significant employment sectors include: education, trade and transportation, government, manufacturing, leisure and hospitality, and professional and business services

- The state student import/export rate in 2002 was 2.98 (they imported 8,701 students and exported 2,919 students; the national rate is 1.19). "For every student we send out of state, we take three back. So we are a poaching state."

Hurry indicated that the Rhode Island Report Card for 2004 served as a wake-up call to the legislature and governor, particularly the "F" in affordability. For the first time in twelve years, they are not cutting back on need-based aid and support for higher education.

Rhode Island Report Card 2004	
Preparation	C+
Participation	A
Affordability	F
Completion	A
Benefits	B+
Learning	I

Hurry sees a major problem in the "C+" in K–12 preparation, and believes more money should be directed there. And while the report card awards an "A" in participation, there has been a 9.7 percent decline since 1992 in the chances of a Rhode Island student enrolling in college by age 19. "Ten years of state budget deficits have led to some tough choices, and it seems that we, like many others, will have to look for other sources of education funding as we go forward."

"If our students graduate from high school, they have an excellent chance of going to college the next fall, and an excellent chance of graduating within six years. But they do this at a price. Clearly, we get an "F" because the percentage of family income needed to pay for college is very high."

Hurry then delineated the access programs that the public institutions have developed. The University of Rhode Island has an articulation and transfer program, a joint admissions agreement, a guaranteed admissions program, special programs for talent development, and the like. Rhode Island College has a duel enrollment program, an articulation and transfer program, Upward Bound, and a preparatory enrollment program for low-income, minority, at-risk, and disabled students, as well as other programs. The Community College of Rhode Island has developed programs that include a high school/community college partnership, and a high school enrichment program; it also participates in joint admissions, articulation, and transfer programs. Hurry noted that the merit-based aid programs at URI and RIC were "worrisome, given declining support for the need-based state grant program at the same time these were being developed." The same amount of funding has gone to these two merit-based programs as has been going to the statewide need-based program.

Statewide initiatives include:

- Rhode Island Children's Crusade
- College Planning Center
- Recent state funding and outreach proposals

Hurry described the very successful Children's Crusade, which was established in 1989 to work with third- through twelfth-graders. They have worked with about 11,000 students; at the moment, 800 are enrolled in higher education. Schools are chosen based on an 80 percent participation rate in the free or reduced-cost lunch program. Third-graders pledge to stay in school, work hard, be good role models, and avoid negative influences and early parenthood. The program has its own board of directors within the Board of Governors for Higher Education and gets funding from the state, a federal GEAR UP grant, corporate and foundation donors, and individuals. A wide variety of services are available to parents and students through this program, including tutoring, homework help, social skills development, and help with the college admissions and financial aid process. Seventy-one institutions in 16 states currently offer scholarships to these students, with an average of five scholarships (generally tuition and fees) per school; all Rhode Island colleges participate in the program.

Hurry briefly mentioned the College Planning Center of Rhode Island, which has five or six outreach centers in malls, schools, and churches, providing financial aid and admissions counseling and materials for all state high schools. The Center also offers an SAT teacher training course at six schools with below-average scores (resulting in an average 89 point increase in scores), and maintains a scholarship Web site.

Hurry's biggest news was the governor's recent doubling of funding (to $10 million) for the Rhode Island State Grant and Scholarship Program, which awards grants based exclusively on financial need. These awards are fully portable to all eligible Title IV institutions. The Rhode Island Higher Education Assistance Authority has added to this with CollegeBound*fund* revenue. CollegeBound*fund*, the state's 529 program, is the second largest in the nation, with much of the money coming from out of state. Its fees generate about $5 million a year to be used for financial aid.

Hurry briefly mentioned a number of initiatives, both ongoing and proposed, that the Rhode Island Higher Education Assistance Authority is involved in, including Rhode Island Scholars, presentations to junior and senior high school classes, New England Dollars for Scholars, College Ready New England, and a regional Web-based outreach system.

Dolores A. Mize, associate vice chancellor and special assistant to the chancellor, Oklahoma State Regents for Higher Education, spoke next about the success they have had in increasing access through the strategic use of public engagement and outreach in Oklahoma. "We have learned that it is important to meet people where they are," Mize said.

Mize described the "silver lining" of Oklahoma having once been a segregated state. To move toward and prove compliance with civil rights requirements, the state developed a comprehensive student database very early on, and thus has a wealth of historical data. One of the findings indicated a high level of math remediation required by students going on to college. The state raised the math requirements for high school students, but also tracked students whom they would like to see in higher education who might not meet the standards. To be sure as many students as possible were prepared for college, a number of interventions were started in the early 1990s, including GEAR UP and the Oklahoma Higher Learning Access Program (OHLAP), about which Mize focused her remarks.

The OHLAP scholarship is available to families with incomes of $50,000 or less (65 percent of families of current high school graduates) who meet academic requirements. An OHLAP scholarship pays the equivalent of public college tuition, but can also be used at private colleges and for some career-tech programs. The scholarship is good for up to five years or the completion of a bachelor's degree, whichever comes first. OHLAP students attend community colleges, four-year regional colleges, and research universities in the state.

Figure 21: OHLAP High School Enrollment By Graduation Year

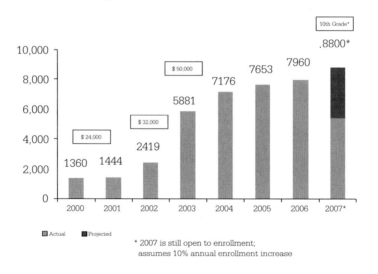

Mize attributes growth in the OHLAP enrollment both to the raising of the family income level cap and the creation of the GEAR UP program. "We were at a critical point with OHLAP; we knew we needed to broaden the awareness of the program, and GEAR UP gave us the means to do so."

Figure 22: OHLAP High School GPAs—All Courses

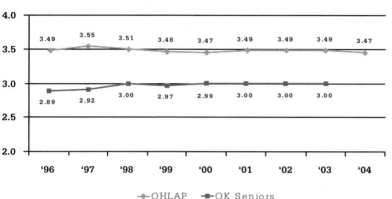

OHLAP students are required to take two more units of study in high school than the minimum required for admission to the state's public institutions. OHLAP set up a minimum of a 2.5 GPA to encourage students in the eighth grade to think they could achieve that—"but they actually average about 3.5." The OHLAP students also generally score better than other students when they take the ACT.

Mize indicated they created their public awareness program with $25 million from GEAR UP. The goals of the campaign were and are to:

- Increase students' educational aspirations
- Increase parents' expectations of educational attainment
- Inform target audiences about preparation required for college
- Correct misperceptions about the cost of college
- Inform target audiences about state and federal financial aid opportunities
- Improve parental involvement in preparing their children for college
- Help teachers and counselors academically prepare their students for college

They began the campaign with a statewide survey. "We needed to be sure that the messages that came out about our program were based on solid data about real Oklahomans." The survey revealed perceived barriers to attending college. Those students planning to attend college were concerned about costs; those not planning to attend college saw their own lack of motivation as a barrier. Parents of students who were not planning to attend college were concerned that their children were not academically prepared.

Building on the results of the survey, the key messages of the outreach campaign were/are:

- Getting a college education is more important now than ever
- It's never too early to start planning for college/talking with your parents/your children about college.
- Money is available to help you pay for college.
- Even if you don't know what career you want to pursue, college can help you explore your options.
- It's easier to go to college right after high school.
- It's good to be the first one in your family to get a college education.

In order to meet students where they are, they worked to create brand identity through logos and "spokesaliens"—developed in part through focus groups of students—that are part of all the OHLAP publicity. Public awareness strategies were developed:

- Instructor's Guide accompanies the video distributed to schools. The guide includes learning objectives, discussion questions, and student activities for students in fifth through seventh grade
- Video for distribution to schools with fifth- through seventh-grade students, as well as to homeschooler associations and academic and community libraries
- Student Activity Booklet, updated each year based on input from teachers and counselors
- Parent Guides direct mailed to parents in three versions: for eighth-grade parents, ninth- and tenth-grade parents, and eleventh- and twelfth-grade parents of students. Guides include information about costs, financial aid, and college preparation
- Use of the Web to reach students, parents, teachers, and counselors
- Posters mailed to 1,300 schools—and there is a free poster on the GEAR UP Web site
- Guide to Oklahoma Colleges and Universities was updated and is available through the Web site and also in print to students without access to the Web
- Paid media:
  - network television: 1,302 television spots aired statewide in a six-week period, reaching 92 percent of all Oklahomans; each person viewed the message an average of 9.7 times
  - cable television: "We ran a six-week campaign only in the areas not served by the network ads"
  - 90 billboards in 30 markets

Mize shared some of the ads that have appeared on television; the key phrase is "Do you?" in response to the statement "I have a plan for college." Students of all ages from fifth through twelfth grade are featured in the ads.

Next, Mize summarized the results to date, based on a 2004 survey to measure the effects of the campaign. A key finding is that the GEAR UP program is working; the advertising program is reaching the people they wanted to reach. Students and parents are now more aware of financial resources and in-state college options. Mize presented the following data summary:

- More parents now think it likely their children will attend college after high school.
- Given that the percentage in the 2000 survey was already high (92 percent), an increase of 2 percent in 2004 is especially meaningful.
- Primary GEAR UP targets (lower income ranges) show the greatest increase of all income segments.
- Oklahoma parents with less education now anticipate more education for their children.
- More two-parent households are likely to expect children to go to college (up 4 percent).
- Fewer single-parent homes think their child will attend a four-year college (down 5 percent). "This tells us where we need to spend time and effort in the next few years."
- For students not planning to got to college, motivation is the key deterrent; money is second.

Mize concluded by saying that GEAR UP has brought college within reach of more students in the past few years. A key growth opportunity lies among parents and students who say the students plan to go to college, but do not matriculate. The next step will be to do a matriculation study, to discover why intentions to attend college do not always result in matriculation.

She shared with the group the number of partners who are helping in the Oklahoma effort (including private banks, supporters of College Goal Sunday, and the Lumina Foundation) and urged the group, "It is important to leverage whatever money you can, from whatever sources, to get the message out. Go find the money if your states are cutting back."

There was no time remaining in this session for audience response.

Federal Law and Financial Aid:

An Overview of the Framework for Evaluating
Diversity-Related Programs

PAM FOWLER, director of financial aid, University of Michigan, led off the session
with thanks to the College Board for pushing to produce financial aid guidance related
to the 2003 Supreme Court ruling on affirmative action. The Access and Diversity
Collaborative (sponsored by 32 colleges as well as 8 educational associations) was launched
in 2004, tackling the topics of financial aid and scholarships, with seminars held around
the country. "National seminars were conducted in New York, Houston, Chicago, and San
Francisco and attracted more than 235 people from 125 institutions. Based on materials
developed for those seminars, and the rich discussions that took place, a strategic planning
and policy manual on federal law and financial aid and scholarships has been drafted. A
prepublication preview of this draft is available today, and the final version is expected in
March."

Fowler shared that work has started on a second topic: outreach, recruitment, retention, and
other student services, with upcoming seminars. She encouraged participating colleges to
send teams of administrators to those seminars, the outcome of which will be a strategic
planning and policy manual on federal law in regard to these services, expected to be
published at the end of the summer of 2005. The Collaborative's final topic, the selection
aspect of admissions, will begin to be addressed with seminars in the fall of 2005.

Art Coleman, attorney, Holland and Knight, LLP, went on to outline the substantive
foundations of federal law with regard to admissions and financial aid that were used as a
basis for the seminar discussions. They include the University of Michigan decisions and
other federal case law, as well as the Department of Education Title VI Policy Guidance
(1994) and Department of Education/ Office of Civil Rights case investigations and
resolutions, which provide nonbinding but illustrative precedents.

Next, Coleman provided a legal overview of the "strict scrutiny" standard. Strict scrutiny
defines the federal inquiry applicable to public or private institutions that receive federal
funds when they condition educational opportunities or benefits based in part or in whole
on race or ethnicity. "The bar is high and the standards are tough. But strict in theory
doesn't mean fatal in fact." He indicated that administrators need to be able to provide the
data and the rationale for race-based financial aid programs at their institutions.

In terms of assessing the risk an institution is exposed to through these policies, Coleman
said, "We are now operating in the context we know, which is admissions; in financial
aid, we are operating in undefined territory, as there was no mention of financial aid
and scholarships in the Michigan decisions. We know a lot of general principles that are
transportable from an admissions context to financial aid, and yet context matters. So you

have to understand the distinctions between financial aid and scholarships on the one hand and admissions on the other before you jump to a cookie-cutter solution. That was the foundation for the College Board initiative, to help define the middle ground."

Coleman then described some of the key issues addressed in the Collaborative meetings around the country:

- How might race-neutral strategies (e.g., socioeconomic status) work to alleviate the need for institution-specific, race-conscious financial aid practices? What research can inform this determination?

- What are the unique features of financial aid that should be considered when evaluating race-neutral alternatives?

- Ways to evaluate the impact of the policy on nonbeneficiaries. What is the percentage of race-conscious aid when examined in light of all other institutional aid and all other institutional non-need-based aid? What is the statistical breakdown (by race, etc.) of all financial aid (including kinds of packaging) provided to students?

Coleman emphasized the importance of process in achieving diversity goals while minimizing legal risk: "for the purposes of federal law, process is substance; and this is one arena where you can get it right; if you do not get the process piece right, you lose." He outlined key action steps to be taken on one's campus:

- *Inventory* "It is crucial to know your program. Gather information regarding all financial aid and scholarship policies that may involve the consideration of race or national origin or that may be diversity related." The inventory should include all types of financial aid and scholarship support, both need- and merit-based; it should also include both institutional and external aid from private, state, and federal sources. Coleman added, "Financial aid cannot and does not operate in a vacuum, so be sure to gather information regarding all related admissions, outreach, and recruitment policies as well."

- *Assemble* "You need to establish an interdisciplinary team to address race-conscious policies. And, although you won't find this point in the federal case law, you do need to obtain a strong institutional commitment, at the highest levels, in support of effective—and lawful—diversity-related policies. In other words, your policies must be mission related." Coleman continued, "You need to assemble a broad team, with healthy tension, so that policy gets clarified. Be sure to include your legal and communications experts on the team along with aid and admissions leaders."

- *Justify* "Do you have clear goals? Do you know what you want to achieve? You need to be able to explain what diversity means: Is it socioeconomic? Disabled students? First-generation? In other words, what type of student body do you want?" Coleman indicated that institutions should ensure that diversity goals are clearly defined with respect to mission-related educational benefits—and that their association with financial aid and scholarship policies is clear. "You need to be able to define when you have achieved diversity and how you know it when you see it. That is a very hard, foundational question. Consider the applicability of a 'critical mass' conceptualization, which the Court embraced; there may be others to consider as well." Institutions should then identify the evidence that supports the justification for each of the relevant policies, using institution-specific evidence, social science research, and opinion evidence.

- **Assess** Coleman emphasized the importance of evaluating the design and operation of policies in light of institutional goals. "Conduct a rigorous evaluation of your race and ethnicity conscious policies in the context of overall objectives and legal standards." Those standards are:

  - Necessity: Is the use of race necessary? Have race neutral policies or strategies been considered or tried?

  - Flexibility: How flexible is the consideration of race? Does it operate as one factor among many? Are there justifications for race-exclusive policies?

  - Burden on nonrecipients: What is the impact of the policy on otherwise qualified nonbeneficiaries?

  - An end in sight and periodic review: Are there durational requirements and a process for review and refinement of the race-conscious policy over time?

- **Act** "Be sure to review outcomes of your diversity efforts and make appropriate adjustments over time. Ensure that the policies are being faithfully executed, and track relevant data points for discussion and evaluation in the context of stated objectives and established policies."

Coleman concluded, "While all of this sounds daunting, it is really no different than Strategic Planning 101. You need to get real institutional focus on the diversity issue. This is about getting to your educational diversity goals. Federal law can actually help institutions make educationally smart and legally sound decisions—if relevant questions are included as part of the strategic planning and policy development process."

He continued, "While many key legal principles are settled, many questions about financial aid and scholarship policies remain—and educators hold many of the answers. Effective institutional planning and analysis can help minimize legal risk without sacrificing core goals. You as institutions have the opportunity to shape the federal policy—if you get this part right. Think of the process not as *against* your institutional goals, but a way to make your efforts better."

The audience then had a chance to respond. Dolores Mize said, "Many federal and quasi-federal agencies continue to have programs that require that institutions give dollars only to racial minorities. What are we to do about these?" Coleman replied, "It is a challenge. Be sure your read of the federal program is accurate—there may be a difference between the ideal objectives and the real *requirements*. There may be some inconsistencies in federal programs. If you think a program exposes you to undue risk, then you need to reconsider and see how relevant it is to the achievement of your goals. This is not about never getting sued, or always winning. You need to understand the relative risk and judge if you can tolerate it or not. I should let you know that I have asked federal agencies about this specific point, requesting information about what their own legal counsels have to say about certain programs; I am awaiting answers."

Dan Goyette, director, office of student financial aid, Marquette University, asked, "Is there any indication of a test case brewing regarding financial aid?" Coleman said, "We do actually know enough from the Michigan case to know what the key questions are and what to do to prepare. I do not know of any test cases brewing, but some 'single shingle' lawyer can always pick up a case. Opponents will probably use the Office of Civil Rights as a precursor to the next stage. It could be years or even decades of cases at the district level before anything gets to the level of the Supreme Court."

Marc Camille, dean of admission, Xavier University, said, "I have a question regarding framing questions as to whether you have achieved diversity goals. If you reach your goals, how do you build the case to sustain what you are doing?" Coleman said, "If you achieve your diversity goals, it does not mean you need to eliminate race-conscious programs. If you reached your goals with those programs, it does not mean you will not need at least some of them to continue. You will just need to make the case on an institution-specific level."

Mayten Sanchez said, "When we speak about diversity there is a large group we tend to ignore: undocumented students. What is being done to address this group's issues?" Coleman relied, "I am not an expert on this issue. Some interpretations of federal law have differed at the state level. Several states on their own have taken steps to allow access or provide tuition waivers for higher education. It is still a muddle. There is a possible opportunity for these students, given labor needs—there may be bipartisan support for a bill by Orrin Hatch to advocate for this group."

Rebecca Dixon stated, "Aside from all these steps you have outlined, there was a bullet point in the draft to 'consider broader public engagement strategies.' I think a lot of us want to stay under the radar. What is meant by that statement? Are we trying to educate the public? Or trying to get the Center for Individual Rights on our case?" Coleman responded, "This statement comes from the college input into the collaborative discussions. You may not want to put your policies on a Web site. The point is that, if this is a mission-driven goal, and you have race-conscious policies to support it, at some level you need to ensure that those issues are understood campuswide, so that people understand. Discuss the difference between affirmative action and quotas. Build institutional awareness to create buy-in. On some campuses, diversity administrators have gone to the business community to build partnerships. Certainly, amicus briefs filed by General Motors, the military, and others in the Michigan case had a direct impact on the victory."

Jim Miller said, "I feel some discomfort among us about what is appropriate in the recruitment process to achieve these goals." Coleman said, "It gets back to doing a thorough inventory of all your programs. Strict scrutiny will apply to all programs when race consciousness leads to a benefit for some students and not others. Recruitment programs that are about expanding the pool of minority students and that are not conferring a benefit per se fall below the strict scrutiny level. There is a big difference between targeting minority schools to try to achieve diversity goals versus running race-exclusive minority weekends on campus."

Dolores Mize said, "Measuring diversity and when we achieve it in terms of inputs and outcomes could have the vestiges of a quota attached to it." Coleman agreed, "Yes, we are between a rock and a hard place. You have to have real, detailed definitions. But you cannot have a definition that is exclusively numbers, because that is a quota. You need to have a set of factors—a framework—that outlines goals in light of the educational benefits to all students."

Bob Lay, dean of enrollment management, Boston College, asked, "What are the dangers of having very specific goals? What about the percentage of representation as a basis for setting goals? The argument would be that we want representation equal to that in society." Coleman answered, "You need to be able to say representation for what purpose? Michigan said it needed better representation to achieve a critical mass, in order for the underrepresented students to feel they could fully participate, and the Supreme Court bought this argument. But to consider '15 percent of the students in my state are Hispanic, so I want 15 percent of my student body to be Hispanic,' I think the court has all but said 'no' to that, as it is too much like a quota and also because the strength of the Michigan case came from what it wanted to do *within* the institution, not looking outward to being the social justice police. They are very interrelated, but the courts do not want you to remedy the outside world."

Pat Coye, director of financial aid, Pomona College, commented, "Some schools at the seminar I attended thought they could use income as the criteria for decision making, but you said that it could also be seen as race conscious. Could you explain that?" Coleman replied, "If it is your goal authentically to have more low-income students, then it does not rise to the level of strict scrutiny. But if you use socioeconomic status as a ruse—your primary motivation is to increase racial and ethnic diversity, and the program works that way, and would not have been implemented without the goal of increasing diversity—there is a fair amount of Supreme Court guidance that suggests, even if it is neutral on its face, it may trigger strict scrutiny. Justice O'Connor dismissed percentage-based programs as an alternative to race-conscious policies, even if they are race neutral."

Mike Scott asked, "What about fraternities and other organizations that are race specific?" Coleman said, "I do not think Justice Scalia's comments in the opinion mean you cannot have clubs or associations that have interests around race or ethnicity. But when an institution closes the doors to whites or blacks in terms of a club, there is a problem. You can have the focus; the issue is whether the door is open to everyone."

The Consequences of Affirmative Action at Selective Institutions

DOUGLAS MASSEY, professor of sociology, Princeton University, told the group that three charges have been leveled at affirmative action:

- The **reverse discrimination hypothesis**, which assumes white applicants are denied admission because less-qualified minority applicants are unfairly admitted. "This is a legal and moral issue more than an empirical issue."

- The **mismatch hypothesis**, which states that lowering admissions standards sets minorities up for failure by placing them in academic settings where they are not prepared; it posits a mismatch between the skills of the student and the skills required for success at selective colleges and universities.

- The **stereotype threat hypothesis**, which posits that affirmative action exacerbates the psychological burden on minority students; that it fuels white perceptions of black intellectual inferiority; that the knowledge that the average black student is less prepared than the average white student heightens racial stigma; and that it affects both how white students view minority students and how minority group members view themselves.

Massey indicated he would be discussing the latter two hypotheses in his remarks, using data from the National Longitudinal Survey of Freshman as a basis for testing them. This information was gathered as a follow-up to *The Shape of the River* (Bowen and Bok). A first volume based on NLSF data has been published, *The Source of the River* (Massey, Charles, Lundy, and Fischer), which he described as an in-depth analysis of the baseline data from the survey, looking at who the students are and what they bring to the beginning of their college experience. Massey said he is working on another volume detailing how their lives unfold as freshmen and sophomores.

"What I am talking about today is a side project, looking at the effect of affirmative action on student performance academically, and on student satisfaction with their college experience. As with many public issues with high emotional content, the ratio of hot air to information is very high. I hope to provide some information to bring that ratio down somewhat."

Massey outlined the design for the study. Howard University, whose data was included in the NLSF, was dropped for this study because the focus is on how minority students fare at largely white institutions. The baseline of students was developed in 1999 as they were about to enter college; and there have been four follow-up telephone interviews—in the spring of 2000, 2001, 2002, and 2003—at the end of each successive college year. The information Massey presented is that through 2002, when the students were juniors in college. At that point, 84 percent of the original cohort responded.

Massey and his colleague, Mary Fischer, had to decide how to measure if students had benefited from affirmative action. They decided to look at how much minority students' SAT scores deviated from the institutional average. "In cases where their scores were above the institutional average, we assumed they were unlikely to be beneficiaries of affirmative action. If their SAT scores were below the institutional average, we suggest there is a possibility that they may have benefited from affirmative action. The further below the institutional average their score, the more likely they are to have been a beneficiary of affirmative action." They also looked at the likelihood that an institution practiced affirmative action, by looking at the minority group test score mean in comparison to the institutional mean. "If a minority group has an average SAT score that is significantly below the institutional average, then we assert that the institution is more heavily using affirmative action criteria."

As for analytic strategy, they considered three outcomes: GPA through the sophomore year, college satisfaction as of the sophomore year, and the probability of leaving school by the end of the junior year. The key predictive variables were the individual level of affirmative action and the institutional level of affirmative action. "If the critics are right, then we would expect to find a relationship between individual affirmative action and these outcomes."

They controlled for a variety of factors, including gender, family socioeconomic status, academic preparation, and social preparation. In terms of measuring satisfaction, they asked students three questions: 1) How satisfied are you with your intellectual development? 2) How satisfied are you with your social life since enrolling? and 3) Considering everything, how satisfied are you with you experience so far?

"In general, Latinos and blacks have lower GPAs than whites; they are less satisfied socially than whites; and that blacks have the highest drop-out rate."

Figure 23: Effect of Individual and Institutional Affirmative Action on Cumulative GPA

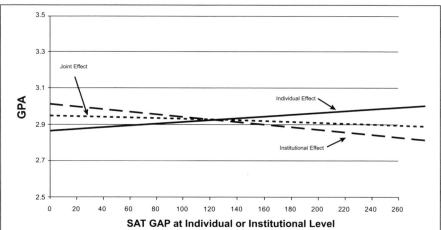

Massey then shared information about the effects of affirmative action on cumulative GPA. "When looking at individual affirmative action, there was no evidence that the students were being set up to fail: in fact, the more the individuals' scores depart from the institutional average, controlling for everything else, the better their performance. We don't know what the mechanism is; maybe they know they are not very well prepared, so they work harder."

In terms of institutional-level affirmative action, they found "significant negative effects on GPA. Maybe when you admit a group of minority students who are perceived to be less able, that will intensify stereotype threat."

Figure 24: Effect of Individual and Institutional Affirmative Action on the Probability of Leaving School

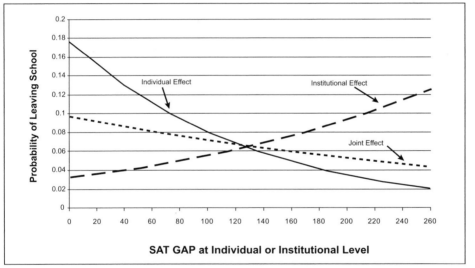

In an aside, Massey looked at legacy and athletic "affirmative action." For the legacies, 7 percent of the sample with whom they were working were sons or daughters of alumni. "This is so low because, in the sample, we surveyed a thousand white, a thousand black, a thousand Asian, and a thousand Latino students, so three-fourths of the sample are non-whites, who are unlikely to be legacies. Of the legacies, 41 percent had SAT scores below the institutonal mean, so they are probably beneficiaries of affirmative action." Athletes made up 9 percent of the survey group, with 59 percent scoring below the institutional average.

"We do not find much effect of legacy affirmative action. At the institutional level, there is no stereotype of the 'dumb legacy student,' and they are not readily identifiable. At the individual level, there is not much effect except on satisfaction—they are less satisfied with their college experience. Athletic affirmative action looks very much like minority affirmative action. At the individual level, there is no evidence that athletes are being set up to fail. However, at the institutional level, we do find negative effects on GPA and satisfaction. So, at institutions where the athletes' scores are significantly below the institutional average, it seems to trigger the same type of stereotype threat as for minority students."

Concluding the part of his remarks about the hypotheses they set out to test, Massey said, "We don't find any evidence for the mismatch hypothesis. Likely beneficiaries of affirmative action actually do better, are more satisfied, and have lower levels of school leaving and a mild improvement in grades. There is some evidence for stereotype threat hypothesis. Minorities seem to do worse in institutions where minority SAT scores are below the institutional average. These two effects are offsetting, and the individual level is generally stronger and dominates in the joint effect."

"Since the big effect here seems to be stereotype threat, I want to unpack that for you," Massey said. He described stereotype threat as a finding developed by Claude Steele and his colleagues at Stanford University, mostly demonstrated using small laboratory experiments. "We wanted to see if we could replicate it and extend the theory using the broad representative sample of students in the NLSF."

Figure 25: Conceptual Model of Effect of Stereotype Threat on Grade Point

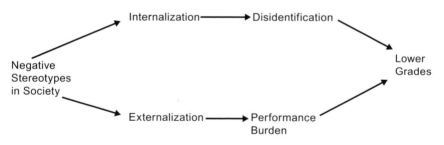

Massey developed this conceptual model. "Negative stereotypes persist, and have two effects on minority students:

1) Negative stereotypes can lead to the internalization of these beliefs in black intellectual inferiority, which can lead to a process of disidentification. If they think they are in danger of confirming the stereotype, they may try less hard; they remove intellectual achievement from their domain of self-worth.

2) Negative stereotypes can lead to externalization: whatever the minority students think on the inside, they also may or may not believe that whites hold negative stereotypes and will be evaluating them on the basis of those stereotypes. This leads to a performance

burden. Whenever they are called upon to perform publicly, they fear, before a white audience, confirming a stereotype, and tend to choke."

Massey said that both of these mechanisms would lead to lower academic achievement.

Massey then described how they measured these effects, by posing the questions, and developing scales to describe the effects.

They developed models predicting

- the degree of internalization of stereotype of intellectual inferiority by black and Latino respondents to the NLSF
- the degree of externalization of stereotype of intellectual inferiority by black and Latino respondents to the NLSF
- the number of hours studied by black and Latino respondents to the NLSF

Figure 26: Model Predicting the Degree of Internalization of Stereotype of Intellectual Inferiority by Black and Latino Respondents to the NLSF

Variable	B	SE
Demographic Background		
Male	0.484*	0.123
Foreign Born Parent	-0.119	0.127
Intact Family Growing Up	0.080	0.149
Number of Siblings<18	0.105	0.070
Socioeconomic Status		
Neither Parent College Graduate	-----	-----
One Parent College Graduate	0.127	0.150
Both Parents College Graduate	-0.250	0.233
One Parent Advanced Degree	0.010	0.016
Both Parents Advanced Degree	-0.172	0.179
Percent of College Paid by Family	0.406*	0.167
Ingroup Exposure		
Segregation Experienced Growing Up	0.000	0.002
% Friends Same Race-Ethnicity	-0.047*	0.040
Racial-Ethnic Identifiers		
Social Distance from Whites	0.011	0.009
Strength of Group Identity	-0.031*	0.015
Skin Color	0.018	0.028
Intercept	6.465 *	0.367
R^2	0.028*	
N	1,619	

* $p < .05$

"Social distance from whites is a big factor here: the degree of exposure that people have had. Those who come from highly educated families and had a lot of exposure to whites, and have a less strong black identity, actually internalize the negative stereotypes more."

Figure 27: Model Predicting the Degree of Externalization of Stereotype of Intellectual Inferiority by Black and Latino Respondents to the NLSF

Variable	B	SE
Demographic Background		
Male	-0.839*	0.244
Foreign Born Parent	-0.142	0.343
Intact Family Growing Up	-0.685*	0.364
Number of Siblings<18	-0.310	0.242
Socioeconomic Status		
Neither Parent College Graduate	----	----
One Parent College Graduate	0.004	0.497
Both Parents College Graduate	0.903 *	0.409
One Parent Advanced Degree	0.727*	0.220
Both Parents Advanced Degree	1.168*	0.445
Percent of College Paid by Family	-0.547	0.579
Ingroup Exposure		
Segregation Experienced Growing Up	-0.015*	0.007
% Friends Same Race-Ethnicity	0.075	0.057
Racial-Ethnic Identifiers		
Social Distance from Whites	0.084*	0.014
Strength of Group Identity	0.181*	0.038
Skin Color	0.224*	0.064
Intercept	18.318*	0.874
R^2	0.088*	
N	1,656	

* $p < .05$

"This indicates the degree to which they expect whites to be judging them on the basis of negative stereotypes. The big factors are having more education, strength of group identity, and darker skin color (which leads them to expect more discrimination).

Figure 28: Model Predicting Hours Studied by Black and Latino Respondents to the NLSF

Variable	B	SE
Internalization of Stereotype		
Internalization Scale	-0.451*	0.139
Demographic Background		
Male	-1.539*	0.901
Foreign Born Parent	1.798*	0.772
Intact Family Growing Up	0.742	0.691
Number of Siblings<18	0.567	0.442
Socioeconomic Status		
Neither Parent College Graduate	----	----
One Parent College Graduate	-0.957	0.914
Both Parents College Graduate	0.019	0.885
One Parent Advanced Degree		
		0.735
		1.008
Both Parents Advanced Degree	-0.001	1.025
Percent of College Paid by Family	-0.241	0.791
Academic Preparation		
Number of AP Courses Taken	0.185	0.185
High School GPA	6.221*	0.947
Self-Rated Preparation	-0.186	0.129
Institutional Selectivity		
Median SAT of School	0.011*	0.005
Intercept	-7.499	7.003
R^2	0.075*	
N		

* $p < .05$

"The effect of interest here is the internalization score, which is highly negative. That is, if you have internalized negative stereotypes about your group's intellectual abilities, you do reduce your work effort and study significantly fewer hours, as Claude Steele would predict. Rather than taking the risk of doing your best on a test and not doing well— thereby confirming to yourself the negative stereotype—you just do not do the work so you have an out.

Figure 29: Model Predicting Performance Burden Felt by Black and Latino Respondents to the NLSF

Variable	B	SE
Externalization of Stereotype		
Externalization Scale	0.129*	0.060
Demographic Background		
Male	1.104*	0.627
Foreign Born Parent	-0.184	0.503
Intact Family Growing Up	0.433	0.562
Number of Siblings<18	0.111	0.269
Socioeconomic Status		
Neither Parent College Graduate	----	----
One Parent College Degree	-0.925	0.694
Both Parents College Graduate	-1.286	1.223
One Parent Advanced Degree	-0.290	0.754
Both Parents Advanced Degree	-1.311	0.779
Percent of College Paid by Family	-1.654*	0.924
Academic Preparation		
Number of AP Courses Taken	0.018	0.126
High School GPA	-1.278	0.671
Self-Rated Preparation	-0.143*	0.078
Institutional Selectivity		
Median SAT of School	0.006	0.003
Intercept	26.023*	5.376
R^2	0.017*	

* $p < .05$

"Again you can see a strong positive effect: to the degree that you expect to be evaluated on the basis of negative stereotypes, you feel a burden when you perform. You feel you are carrying the entire group on your back.

"These two factors, studying less and experiencing performance burden, have strong effects on grade point average. As you study less, your grade point falls. As your psychological performance burden increases, your grade point falls.

"So basically, we confirmed the conceptual model. Negative stereotypes in society lead to processes of internalization and externalization of stereotypes. Internalization does produce disidentification, which translates directly into lower grades. Likewise, externalization leads to a performance burden which, again, translates into lower grades."

Massey concluded that, in terms of affirmative action, there is no evidence that students are set up to fail. Individually they do as well or better in comparison to other students. "But when an institution employs affirmative action criteria, they may inadvertently heighten stereotype threat. And when we explore stereotype threat, we find that the mechanisms that have been postulated, by Claude Steele and others, on the basis of small laboratory studies do appear to operate in theoretically expected ways in a large sample of students across a variety of institutions.

"Does this mean that we should not use affirmative action because it may exacerbate stereotype threat? Not necessarily. Claude Steele, in an article that will appear in the *Harvard Education Review*, does what he calls 'a wise intervention' at the University of Michigan. He shows that you can completely get rid of the stereotype effects for a sample of students if you structure your programs to de-emphasize the racial stigma. Steele took a sample of students and organized them into study groups and rather than saying they were getting remedial treatment, told them they were getting special treatment. By presenting it and having it perceived not as making up for deficiencies, but as rewarding ability, the students performed superlatively and it got rid of the stereotype effect."

According to Massey, another option that is within an institution's control is minority representation on the faculty.

Figure 30: Model Predicting GPA Earned by Respondents to the NLSF During First Three Terms of College or University: High and Low Representation of Minority Faculty

	Low Minority Representation on Faculty		High Minority Representation on Faculty	
Variable	B	SE	B	SE
Theoretical Predictor				
Hours Studied Per Week	0.002*	0.001	0.003*	0.001
Performance Burden	-0.002*	0.001	0.000	0.001

* $p < .05$

"Performance burden only crops up as a significant effect when there is low minority representation on the faculty. High representation of minority faculty leads to no effect."

Massey concluded that, although institutional practice of affirmative action can exacerbate stereotype threat effects, there are actions colleges and universities can take to mitigate those effects. He indicated that the stereotype threat research, conducted jointly with Mary J. Fischer of the University of Connecticut, would appear in the next issue of the *DuBois Review*.

The audience then had a chance to respond. Anna Marie Porras, director of admission, Stanford University, said, "When you use the SAT mean as the cutoff, you are using a mean that is already being driven down by the subpopulations you are studying. I am also struggling with the use of the SAT in a way that it should not be used in a selective college process. To define someone as a beneficiary of affirmative action because their score falls below the mean is a bit of a stretch for me." Massey replied, "On the first point, it would probably be better to use SAT scores disaggregated by race, but while all colleges publish a mean, they do not all publish disaggregated data. We hope to have such data in the future. And I agree it is a stretch to use the scores this way, but I chose them because everyone focuses on the SAT. When people talk about unqualified students coming in, the first thing they focus on is SAT scores. That's where the public debate is. If you have a better gauge, we would be very interested."

Bob Lay asked, "Is there something between the individual and institutional effects of affirmative action: what about group effects? When you bring in more students below the mean, you are also changing the group dynamics within the institution. An alternate explanation for what you have presented today is that an institution that brings in larger numbers of lower scoring students may be creating a larger support group. That may explain why there is a higher retention rate, and it may be more socially acceptable to take a slight drop in GPA in order to be mutually supported." Massey agreed, "I don't know that it's an alternate explanation—it is an explanation for the effect. Students are not being set up to fail, and this may be a reasonable explanation. It would be consistent with what happens with the athletes, that they bond and support each other; and institutions also intervene to be sure their athletes do not fail. We will start reviewing these 28 institutions' policies and measuring how they intervene in these basic processes."

Rick Lamberson, assistant director of admissions, New College of Florida, asked, "Were there differences in terms of the findings at institutions with fewer than 100 minority students?" Massey replied, "We didn't look at it that way. But the baseline data will be up in a month for public review on the NLSF Web site, so that you can look at it for yourself."

Bruce Poch, vice president and dean of admissions, Pomona College, said, "Your baseline assumes white is normative. I am concerned that the vocabulary for what is normative may not be the case for some of these institutions." Massey replied, "The baseline is the institutional average, not the white average. I have referred throughout the talk to the departure from the institutional average, because that is what was studied."

Youlonda Copeland-Morgan asked, "Were there surprises in your research and other research questions that came out of this study?" Massey said, "There are always surprises and more questions. Another line of work that we have published in a set of papers is focused on the long-term effects of segregation. We are still a residentially segregated society. The neighborhoods where some of the students in our study grew up are different from those of others. Their social networks extend back to those neighborhoods. It is not a level playing field. Things happen within their social networks of racially segregated students that detract from their college performance. They are more likely than white students to have friends or relatives get injured or killed, more likely to have people in their social networks in trouble with the law. A significant percentage of these students, even though they are financially disadvantaged in comparison to other students on campus, are sending money home. They spend more time off campus attending to these problems, and spend more energy on them. In 2000, half of all urban African Americans lived in metropolitan areas so segregated that the only comparison is South Africa under apartheid. This has continuing consequences. We have not equalized disadvantaged minority students' chances by bringing them to these institutions. The pressures every college student faces are worse for minority students and, in addition, there are pressures that only they experience. And these are effects they can't control. Our next book will show how all this plays out in their freshman and sophomore years."

Erica O'Neal, assistant vice president of student affairs, California Institute of Technology, said, "You indicated that we could mitigate stereotype threat by getting more minority faculty, but that is even harder than getting the students. Are there other mitigating factors that we could explore?" Massey responded, "That is the only one we have identified so far. We will look at other institutional level effects in future research. I do understand how difficult it is to recruit minority faculty—but we can't let up."

Rebecca Dixon asked, "In terms of the gender of minority students in college, two-thirds are women. Did you look at your African American data by gender?" Massey said, "We suspect many of these processes are gender specific, and Mary Fischer is looking at some of that right now. One of our surprises in the first book was the 2:1 ratio of black women to black men in our survey. This exacerbates the issues around romance and dating and love on campus, which are intensified for black college women. Black women face a very difficult situation: within the black elite, half will remain single, or will have to cross class or racial lines. If this ratio is perpetuated year after year in the colleges, it will create a huge demographic imbalance."

Tom McWhertor, vice president for enrollment and external relations, Calvin College, said, "I am still stuck on the use of median SAT. Might it still be profitable to look at the middle 50 percent as the dividing line, and look at affirmative action level at the below 25 percent area? It might demonstrate more appropriately how we use test scores." Massey replied, "We did think about this, and how to measure affirmative action. We thought about using the bottom quartile, but that seemed to reify SAT scores even more. So we decided to use the scores as a continuous variable."

Refocusing on the Common Good

JAMES MONTOYA, vice president for regions and higher education services, the College Board, gave the Colloquium wrap-up. He said, "I would like to share a few reflections on what we have heard, and I will start with what Andre Bell said, that our democratic ideals are related to equity and access. Yet a lot of what I have heard during the panel discussions points out the tension between democracy and our capitalistic framework. Those words that we most associate with democracy—broad participation, social benefits, multiple winners—are in contrast with those we identify with a capitalistic framework—economic engine, competition, personal benefits, winners, and losers."

Montoya expressed concern that we do not have a shared notion of the common good. But he believes there are some common qualities that fit with both democracy and capitalism: ingenuity, social mobility, opportunity, and empowerment. "It is important that we capture those qualities and allow them to establish common ground as we move forward to establish a definition of common good. The demographic information we received should be very helpful in doing that."

Montoya then shared what surprised him over the course of the Colloquium. "Much of the information we have heard before, in different ways. So I was not surprised with Dr. Tobin's information from the Mellon study that students from the top quarter of socioeconomic status are six times more likely to go to college than those in the bottom quarter. But I was surprised that nonminority, high-achieving students from low-SES families were not admitted at a higher rate than those in higher income groups. That led me to think about what Art Coleman said about our own sense of what diversity is—how we are guided by a visible sense of diversity, that somehow those who are visibly and identifiably different lend more diversity to our campuses.

"There were a few moments when I wish I had spoken up. One was during Randy Swing's presentation, when he asked if the retention figures looked bad. The reaction most of us had was that they looked better than we expected. After six years, 63 percent graduated; 20 percent had no degree and were no longer enrolled. After reflection, I was thinking about that 20 percent who started—with the presumed goal of graduating—and did not finish. It made me think of how many students we lose along the continuum: the thought of losing another 20 percent is rather frightening to me." He urged the group to think about these national statistics: only 38 percent of last year's ninth-graders will go on to any form of higher education. "And then we lose another 20 percent of those we would most like to keep in higher education—those at four-year colleges.

"I also thought about the important role of community colleges. Many speakers referred to them. This is an opportunity for all of us to think about our relationships with community colleges, and to fully embrace and understand the key role they will play as demographics bring many more Latino, African American, and Asian American students to higher education. We can have an impact in ensuring their greater success."

Montoya shared when he had felt most optimistic. "One of those moments came when Don Saleh spoke of reaching those who were much younger, who were in the sixth grade—and knowing that the College Board was already working and expanding in those areas with programs like SpringBoard™.

"What will I take away with me? First, a stronger commitment to that bridge between K–12 and higher education, understanding the role of preparation as it relates to admissions and retention; and recognition that college success is a concept that does not simply belong to colleges but to K–12 as well. Second, a sense that we must be much more vocal about what defines the common good. We are in a wonderful position to do this: people actually listen to us regarding what the value of college is and, more importantly, who should be in college. We are already doing this, but it is important to have a common vocabulary and a common vision.

"It has become clear to me that the common good, a values-driven concept, must be fueled by our uncommon commitment to advancing equity and access. I leave here asking, 'What can I do? What will I do?' We all agree we must do something. I look forward to working with all of you as we move ahead."

Appendix A

The "Supply-Side Block" in Higher Education:
Attainment, Equity, and Social Class

Keynote Address by Eugene Tobin

The editors of the *Economist* recently observed that "the United States likes to think of itself as the very embodiment of meritocracy: a country where people are judged on their individual abilities rather than their family connections…" To be sure, the editors observed, "America has often betrayed its fine ideals…yet…today most Americans believe that their country still does a reasonable job of providing opportunities for everybody…But are they right?…The education system is increasingly stratified by social class, and poor children have a double disadvantage. They attend public schools with fewer resources than those of their richer contemporaries. And America's great universities," according to the *Economist*, "are increasingly reinforcing rather than reducing these educational inequalities." [1]

I hope my comments will shed some light on these themes and stimulate and contribute to our conversation during the next two days. I am eager to learn from all of you as we move through a very interesting collection of sessions led by some very talented and interesting speakers.

Each year around this time the members of the Judson Welliver Society, the association of former White House speechwriters, holds its annual dinner at a trendy Washington, D.C., restaurant. I'm told that you can actually hear a low buzz in the room between after-dinner toasts. It is the distinguished membership murmuring the mantra "Tell them what you're going to tell them; then tell them; then tell them what you've told them." [2]

So—I'm going to begin with a contemporary overview of current attitudes and concerns regarding higher education; then I'll briefly trace some historical parallels examining issues of equity and exclusion, before moving up to the present with a macroanalysis of how higher education has handled equity concerns at the national level. The centerpiece of my remarks focuses on data and findings drawn from 19 selective public and private institutions, part of the research for a new book, *Equity and Excellence in American Higher Education* (University of Virginia Press, 2005), which allows my coauthors, William Bowen and Martin Kurzweil, and me to share some thoughts about the experiences of five special groups of applicants to these institutions—underrepresented minorities, recruited athletes, students from low-income and first-generation college families, legacies, and early decision/early action candidates.

Finally, in conclusion, three words described by a colleague as among the most beautiful in the English language, I will suggest some ideas for how we might close the "preparation" gap and break open the "supply-side block" that currently impede access to the nation's most selective colleges for students from disadvantaged socioeconomic backgrounds.

Attitudes Toward Higher Education

Americans feel very positively about the quality of their colleges and universities. A 2004 survey found that 93 percent of respondents consider our colleges and universities to be "one of the [country's] most valuable resources." [3] Survey respondents are much more ambivalent, however, about how and to whom access to these "valuable resources" should be provided.

A robust majority worry that colleges are too expensive, and many parents express concern about being able to afford their children's education. Moreover, admissions policies that veer from the consideration of "objective" measures like SAT scores and grades are viewed with skepticism—three-quarters of respondents disapproved of legacy preferences, and the nation is about evenly divided on the question of affirmative action for racial and ethnic minorities. [4]

There has long been a simmering debate in this country over whether it is better to educate a small number of people to a very high standard or to extend educational opportunities much more broadly—even if this means accepting a somewhat lower standard of performance and, in general, spreading resources more thinly. There has also been a more pointed debate, dating back to the early nineteenth century, over efforts to admit students from a wide variety of cultural, socioeconomic, and religious backgrounds. [5]

First, there were the "poor but hopeful[l] scholars" from the New England countryside, those whom Harvard historian Samuel Eliot Morison famously called the "horny-handed lads from country districts" [6]; these were young men, usually the younger, ambitious sons of farm families, who left the limited opportunities of an overcrowded agricultural sector behind and invested their hopes in a college education. Many had been inspired by the religious revivals of the Second Great Awakening and worked their way through New England's gentlemen colleges primarily to enter the ministry and other emerging professions.

During the 1820s and 1830s, the so-called "Age of the Common Man," the education of women became a contentious and controversial subject, first in female academies and seminaries, then in women's colleges and still later in coeducational institutions as women, inspired by the abolitionist and women's rights movements, sought access to full citizenship through participation in higher education.

In the late nineteenth and early twentieth centuries, America's higher education leaders "deliberately, self-consciously, and articulately manipulated" admissions policies to preserve a social order they correctly believed was under siege from the sons and daughters of the so-called "new immigrants" from Southern and Eastern Europe.[7] During these years, Congress passed immigration restriction laws and many colleges and universities introduced admissions quotas to limit the number of Jewish and, in some cases, Catholic students in their student bodies.

In the American South, the end of Reconstruction led to systematic segregation under Jim Crow, and the introduction of separate and unequal educational facilities. North of the Mason-Dixon line, de facto segregation and exclusionary admissions policies proved equally effective in limiting opportunities for African Americans.

Today's barriers to entry are vastly different. Although explicit policies to keep certain people out have been eliminated, more "organic" barriers—such as poor academic and social preparedness, information deficits, and outright financial hardship—are limiting college opportunities for students from socioeconomically disadvantaged backgrounds—a group that contains more white students than minority students, even though racial minorities are disproportionately represented. These barriers are just as troublesome in their effects and in many ways more difficult to overcome than the explicit exclusion of individuals with unwanted characteristics.

By the mid-1960s, stimulated by the Civil Rights Movement, many colleges and universities began to recruit minority students, first haltingly, and then much more aggressively. In retrospect, it's easy to assume that these changes in admissions policies were accomplished without difficulty. But this was certainly not the case at Yale, where President Kingman Brewster's appointment of R. Inslee Clark as director of admissions in 1965 provoked a debate within the Yale Corporation that is almost unimaginable today. Here is a short account from Geoffrey Kabaservice's recent book, *The Guardians*, of a spring 1966 meeting in which Dean Clark made his first report to Yale's trustees on his efforts to diversify the incoming class, and was vigorously questioned by a skeptical board member:

> Let me get down to basics, you're admitting an entirely different class than we're used to. You're admitting them for a different purpose than training leaders.' Unspoken but understood by all, was that the dean of admissions' new emphasis had rejected unprecedented numbers of wealthy, WASP applicants from preparatory schools, many of them alumni sons, who had been Yale's longtime constituency. Clark responded that in a changing America, leaders might come from nontraditional sources, including public high school graduates, Jews, minorities, even women. His interlocutor shot back, 'You're talking about Jews and public school graduates as leaders. Look around you at this table'—he waved a hand at [President] Brewster, Lindsay, Moore, Bill Bundy, and other distinguished men assembled there. 'These are America's leaders. There are no Jews here. There are no public school graduates here. [8]

Needless to say, there were no African American members of the Yale Corporation in 1966. Nonetheless, Brewster, Clark, and Yale persevered and provided visible leadership in overturning long-held presumptions about who did and did not "belong" at selective colleges and universities. Today, we face a different set of challenges.

College Enrollment

Overall, college enrollment rates have increased for all racial, ethnic, and socioeconomic (or SES) groups over the last 30 years. Increases in real income, in student aid, and in the returns to college education have combined to produce this welcome result. But the fact that enrollment rates have gone up "across the board" does not mean that there is anything like equal access to college today. The different SES groups started at different levels and so, in the words of a recent College Board report: "An individual's chances of entering . . . college remain closely correlated with family background" and a host of factors we group under the name of "college preparedness." [9]

As a general rule, families that have high incomes and high educational attainment when their children are of college age had high incomes and high educational attainment when their children were young, and these persistent advantages enabled them to enhance the "college preparedness" of their children in reinforcing ways. We know that students from high-income families (and families with high educational attainment) are encouraged to think about college, to take college-preparatory courses, and to ready themselves to take the SATs and other tests used to assess college applicants.

One useful benchmark of this mindset is that students from well-to-do families are far more likely than students from lower SES categories to take the SAT in the first place. And test-takers from families with high incomes and high educational attainment do much better on the SATs than do students from less affluent families.

Our analysis of data drawn from the National Educational Longitudinal Study (NELS) demonstrates the dramatic advantages associated with coming from a high SES family. The odds of taking the SAT and scoring over 1200 are roughly *six* times higher for students from the top-income quartile than for students from the bottom-income quartile; and those odds are roughly *seven* times higher for students from the top-income quartile than for students who are from the bottom-income quartile *and* who are also the first in their families to attend college. [10]

The "Supply-Side Block"

The fact that many high school students from low socioeconomic status families are qualified for college but do not attend, or go to colleges that are less selective than their achievements justify, is not widely recognized beyond the higher education community. "Low-income and working-class students of all colors," as Richard Kahlenberg has observed, "constitute America's great untapped resource." [11] This is true for nonminority students from working-class and impoverished backgrounds who have not been affected by race-sensitive affirmative action programs, and it is also true for underrepresented minority students who have not been part of the competitive bidding war created by affirmative recruiting, and who are capable of doing much better than their modest grades and test scores would predict.

The primary cause of this "untapped resource" is a "supply-side" block that threatens this country's growth in educational attainment—and which exists in spite of rising economic returns to education. An academic preparedness gap starts almost at birth, continues through adolescence, and is shaped by students' in-school and out-of-school environment. The inequities that dampen aspiration and academic development for students who live on the edge of urban and rural poverty begin immediately and reflect accumulating disadvantages ranging from inadequate prenatal care to family instability, income disparities, unsafe neighborhoods, a lack of adult role models, and deficient, underfunded educational programs beginning with preprimary and extending through high school.

Income, Information, and Sophistication

Most economists agree that so-called short-term "credit constraints" matter, and that they would matter much more in the absence of the well-developed financial aid programs in America today. However, the number of students who are currently prevented from enrolling in college by a straightforward inability to pay is small—economists Pedro Carneiro and James Heckman estimate that fewer than 8 percent of students fall into this category.[12] Still, higher income families obviously have an easier time "paying the bills." Moreover, parents with high educational attainment also foster college enrollment after the test score results are known by providing guidance, contacts, and knowledge about how the "admissions game" works. Our research suggests that family finances have a fairly minor direct impact on a student's ability to attend a college (because of relatively low costs at less selective colleges and generous financial aid at more selective colleges), but family finances are extremely important in developing the academic preparedness, practical knowledge, and skills that enable students to attend. It is these myriad, interconnected, deep-seated, and long-lasting effects of socioeconomic status that make the educational opportunity gap so persistent—and so hard to close.[13]

College Attainment Versus College Enrollment

The differential college graduation rates of low- and high-income students, and of minority and nonminorities, exceed differences in enrollment rates and add another layer of complexity to the discussion of equity in educational opportunity. For 1992 high school graduates who started at a four-year institution, there is a 34-percentage-point difference in bachelor's degree attainment between those in the lowest income quartile (44.2 percent) and those in the top-income quartile (78.2 percent).[14] There is also a large (roughly 15-percentage-point) gap in degree attainment between blacks and whites—and this gap has not closed at all over the past 50 years.[15]

Moreover, although college enrollment has risen over the past 30 years for all groups, economist Sarah Turner finds that the college completion rate has declined among those in their early twenties and stagnated for those in their early thirties, indicating that attainment rates have stalled while time-to-degree has unambiguously increased over the last three decades.[16] Policies that encourage enrollment ("access") for all but then fail to provide the guidance and resources that allow students to translate participation into timely attainment—especially students who come from lower income families—are in many ways a waste of both public and personal resources. As Turner points out, the private financial returns to college education accrue mainly to those who earn degrees, and the returns are highest for those who earn their degrees quickly.[17]

Here we have an important question for public policy: Would it be wiser to invest more resources in the education of continuing student populations than in simply embracing access as an end in itself? My colleagues and I sit firmly in the camp of those who argue that the progress of current students toward their degree should not be underemphasized. There is much to be said for allocating funds to institutions that bear the brunt of rising enrollments. We should help these institutions meet the legitimate educational needs of larger populations of students who may not be able to complete their college degrees without considerable assistance. The dictates of basic fairness as well as considerations of economic efficiency also argue strongly for improving the college preparedness of the marginal students whose quest for a college degree may be frustrated, not at the college gate, but after having passed through it.

College Choice

Perhaps the most complicated set of facts are those linked to college choice. There is no question that low-income students are underenrolling in the most selective, most expensive institutions, even after controlling for their college preparedness and other observable characteristics. Given the disproportionately high benefits that the selective schools offer, this is a troubling finding. What explains it? Are these institutions simply too expensive for low-income college-goers? Is the true capacity of these students to do first-rate academic work unappreciated or unobserved? Do they underapply, are they underadmitted, or do they fail to matriculate if admitted? Are the selective colleges and universities making sufficient efforts to help these students attend their institutions and graduate from them? Let's turn now to a few of these questions.

Thanks to the cooperation of 19 highly selective colleges and universities, and to the assistance of the College Board, which helped us link institutional records provided by individual schools to the wealth of data about family backgrounds, test scores, and the like provided in the Student Descriptive Questionnaire filled out by all students who take the SAT, we now have at our disposal a rich new data set. This data set allows us to look "microscopically" at the more than 180,000 applications to these schools for places in the 1995 entering cohort, at the characteristics of those applicants offered admission, at the yields on those offers and, finally, at the performance of the matriculants themselves as they moved through college to graduation.[18]

The fundamental question is whether these highly regarded institutions should today be considered "engines of opportunity" or "bastions of privilege." The president of one of them posed a central question to us early on this project: "In applying to my university, is an applicant better off, other things equal, being rich or poor?" Put another way: Is there an admissions advantage associated with being poor, or with being the first member of your family to go to college, that is comparable to the advantage associated with being a minority student, a legacy, or a recruited athlete? Let me summarize our conclusions with some broad-brush strokes.

First, the percentage of students from bottom-income quartile families and the percentage who are first-generation college students are both small. Students whose families are in the bottom quartile of the national income distribution represent roughly 11 percent of all students at these 19 schools, and first-generation college students represent a little over percent of these student populations. Nationally, of course, the bottom-income quartile is—by definition—25 percent of the population, while 38 percent of the national population of 16-year-olds have parents who never attended college.[19] Both these groups are heavily underrepresented at the institutions in our study. When we combine the two measures of SES, and estimate the fraction of the enrollment at these schools that is made up of students who are both first-generation college-goers and from low-income families, we get figure of about 3 percent.[20] Nationally, the share of the same-age population who fell into this category was around 19 percent in 1992, making this doubly disadvantaged group even more underrepresented than students with just one of the two characteristics.[21]

The second main conclusion, which may surprise you, is that these percentages do not change very much as we move from the applicant pool to the group of students admitted, to those who enroll, and finally to those who graduate. This consistent pattern suggests that socioeconomic status does not affect progression through these stages, which leads to a third finding we consider especially striking.

Once disadvantaged students make it into the credible applicant pool of one of these highly selective schools (no easy accomplishment to be sure), they have essentially the same experiences as their more advantaged peers.[22]

There is, naturally enough, some variation among our 19 institutions. As one might expect, the share of enrolled students from the bottom-income quartile is slightly higher at the public universities than at the private colleges and universities (11.8 percent versus 0.6 percent), as is the share that are first-generation college-goers (8.8 percent versus 5 percent). But these differences are hardly dramatic and reflect the high degree of selectivity of all these schools, and the strong correlation between SATs and socioeconomic status. This is particularly true of students at the four flagship public universities in our study—(UCLA, the University of Virginia, the University of Illinois, and Penn State) where top-income quartile students with parental incomes of at least $200,000 outnumber students whose parents make less than the national medium of about $53,000. Only 4 percent of all students at the public universities are both first-generation college-goers and from low-income families, compared with just fewer than 3 percent at the private institutions.[23]

Admissions

The question of admissions preference needs to be addressed directly and our data allow us to do this across the distribution of SAT scores by income and race. I should note that the distribution of SAT scores is more closely correlated with race than it is with income. We found that even within the highly select population of students in the applicant pools of these 19 colleges and universities, SAT scores vary markedly according to family income and parental education. Average (combined) SAT scores of applicants are, for the most part well over 100 points lower for applicants from families in the bottom-income quartile or those with no parental history of college attendance.

When we examined admissions probabilities for three groups of applicants—nonminority students from bottom-quartile families, first-generation nonminority students, and all other applicants (of higher SES) who are not members of underrepresented minority groups—and holding SAT scores constant, there is virtually no difference in the chances of being admitted, at any SAT level, for students from the two low-SES categories and for all other (nonminority) students.

Equally noteworthy is the clear finding that, while applicants from families in the bottom-income quartile get no help in admissions, on an other-things-equal basis, neither do applicants from the families in the top quartile of the income distribution. Most of the 19 institutions in our study claim to be "need-blind" in admissions—to pay no attention whatsoever to the financial circumstances of their applicants. And our data suggest that in fact they are need-blind.[24]

Admissions Advantages for "Special Groups"

The adjusted admissions advantage enjoyed by four groups of "special" applicants—recruited athletes, minority students, legacies, and early action/early decision candidates—are far greater, in an other-things-equal basis, than the advantage of 4.1 points enjoyed by first-generation college students.

Recruited athletes receive the biggest boost at these institutions, about 30 percentage points, followed by underrepresented minorities at 28 points, legacies at about 20 points, and early action/early decision candidates also at about 20 points. In general, an applicant with an admissions probability of, say, 40 percent based on SAT scores and other variables would have an admissions probability of 70 percent if he or she were a recruited athlete, 68 percent if a member of an underrepresented minority group, and 60 percent if a legacy or an early action/early decision applicant. The reasons for giving admissions advantages to these four groups are, of course, radically different, and I will return to that question momentarily.[25] But first, I want to say something about academic performance at these 19 institutions.

Academic Underperformance

Earlier research done by colleagues at the Mellon Foundation and presented in William Bowen and Derek Bok's seminal study, *The Shape of the River*, and in Bowen and Sarah Levin's *Reclaiming the Game* has shown that minority students earn lower grades than we would expect them to earn based on their SAT scores, fields of study, and high school grades.[26] This phenomenon, which we refer to as "underperformance," is evident to an even greater extent among recruited athletes than among minority students. Do students from disadvantaged backgrounds also "underperform?" The simple (perhaps surprising, but very encouraging answer): *They do not. Students from low-income and low parental education families do not exhibit any significant underperformance; they do almost exactly as well as we would expect them to do.* This important finding can be compared to the approximately 9-percentile-point underperformance of minority students and the 10-point underperformance of recruited athletes at the schools in our study.

Cutting through all of our analysis, there is one major takeaway: for those applicants who took the SAT, did well on it, and applied to one of these selective institutions, family income and parental education, in and of themselves, had surprisingly little effect on admissions probabilities, on matriculation decisions, on choices of majors, on subsequent academic performance and graduation rates, and even on later-life outcomes such as earnings and civic participation. This is not to say that socioeconomic status has little or no effect on college enrollment and degree attainment at these academically selective schools, or on lifetime earnings and other outcomes. It has had (and still has) a huge effect. But "the effect" occurs early on, in the years before college application, when "preparedness" is shaped through the persistent, cumulative development of cognitive skills, motivation, expectations, and other noncognitive qualities; and the practical knowledge about the college admissions process.

When well-prepared applicants from poor families, or from families without prior college experience appear in applicant pools (often as a result of the efforts of dedicated parents and teachers, as well as aggressive recruiting by the colleges and universities), these candidates are treated in admissions in very much the same way as everyone else. And, once enrolled, they then perform, as they would be expected to perform. *But the odds of getting into this highly competitive pool in the first place depend enormously on who you are and how you grew up.*

Given this reality, one key question arises: Are the claims of "equity" really being met through a need-blind approach in a society in which students are so stratified by socioeconomic status in their precollege years?

Although early decision applicants, legacies, underrepresented minorities, and recruited athletes are anywhere from 20 percentage points to 30 percentage points more likely to be admitted than otherwise similar applicants, candidates from low-income backgrounds, and those who would be the first in their families to attend college have an admission rate that is virtually identical to that of more privileged applicants with the same test scores, grades, race, and other characteristics. These students clearly are not receiving any kind of "admissions advantage"; at the same time, they are not being penalized for their disadvantaged backgrounds, as some have suggested.

The question for presidents, administrative officers, faculty, and trustees responsible for setting policy can be simply stated: looking ahead, is this set of preferences the best way to allocate scarce places at highly selective institutions? Needless to say, the reasons for giving preferences to various groups differ radically, and we believe that some justifications are much more persuasive than others.[27]

First, minority preferences serve several basic educational and societal goals, including, as the Supreme Court noted in *Grutter v. Bollinger*, a diverse student body provides educational benefits to all students. Race matters in America and that reality needs to be acknowledged in terms of the racial stigmas that profoundly disadvantage minority students.

Legacy preferences serve to enhance the ties of alumni to their alma mater. Schools have an understandable interest in keeping their alumni feeling positively about their institutions. Alumni children are expected to carry historical ties and commitments into a new day and, of course, colleges and universities rely heavily on alumni donations for discretionary funding and capital campaign projects that improve the environment for all students and faculty. In our view, there is a clear trade-off between the goals of equity (which are not advanced by preferences of this kind) and the goals of excellence (which do depend on generating resources from alumni and other donors). But to make the excellence argument, it is necessary that legacy and development preferences be conferred with something approaching surgical precision, and that great care be taken in deciding how much of a "break" to give which candidates, and that the numbers not be too large.

Whereas minority admissions preferences serve educational and societal purposes, and legacy/development preferences serve institutional purposes, the preferences given to recruited athletes serve primarily the narrower purposes of the institution's athletic establishment and the interests of trustees and alumni with strong feelings about athletics. Recent research reveals all too clearly the ways in which intercollegiate athletics conflicts with core academic values at many of the nation's most selective colleges that do not offer athletic scholarships. It seems evident that athletic preferences raise fundamental questions about core commitments, resource allocations—and about what matters most in crafting an incoming class. The fact that recruited athletes underperform academically whether they play or not, also suggests real limitations on continuing these forms of preference.[28]

Although they are not defined by demographic characteristics or by their interest in a particular activity such as varsity sports, early decision applicants can also be considered a "special group" from the standpoint of admissions preferences. Our data confirms the findings of other scholars that students who apply early enjoy a decided admissions advantage. We recognize that early decision and early action programs are valued by prospective students who definitely know where they want to go and wish to be spared the agony of waiting until spring. From a larger perspective, what is most troubling about this form of preference is that it rewards applicants (and secondary schools) who are fortunate enough to know that applying early can benefit them substantially. The very nature of these programs –which require students offered admission to matriculate at the school in question—makes it impossible for students who have financial need to compare financial aid offers from various schools in which they are interested. (Minority students are, of course, disproportionately represented in the "need-sensitive" category.) These programs also encourage the applicants and the institution to "game" the system—allowing candidates to apply early to a second choice school (assuming it's less selective than the candidate's first choice) and allowing the college or university to improve its yield, thereby lowering its acceptance rate.

Our own biases lean toward admissions policies that strengthen the complementarities between excellence and equity. Thus, among these four privileged groups, my colleagues and I are most comfortable supporting minority preferences (because of the educational and societal goals to which diversity contributes), and we are least comfortable rationing highly desirable places at selective institutions to students whose athletic abilities serve narrower interests.

But before one can benefit from an admissions advantage, there is an even bigger hurdle— getting into the "credible" applicant pool. Getting into this pool depends to a great degree on one's race and on how one grew up. As I've suggested—here's the "tell them what you've told them" part of my remarks—our research demonstrates that the odds of being in this applicant pool are *six* times higher for a student from a high-income family than for a student from a poor family; and they are *seven* times higher for an applicant from a college-educated family than they are for a student who is a first-generation college-goer. But once disadvantaged students make it into the credible pool, they have essentially the same odds of admission (given their SAT scores and other credentials) as do other applicants, and their subsequent experiences mirror those of their more privileged classmates.

In spite of strenuous efforts by these 19 selective institutions, especially in their affirmative recruitment of underrepresented minorities—efforts that must continue—additional steps are urgently needed to address the needs of all qualified students from disadvantaged backgrounds. Simply put, poor families have greater difficulty than more affluent families investing sufficient personal and financial resources to encourage their children's abilities and inclinations to attend college, do well, and graduate. These "preparedness" gaps are due to a variety of interacting causes, from inadequate health care to neighborhood quality to poor schools plagued by limited funding and other accumulating disadvantages that dampen aspiration and academic advancement. The only way to fix this problem in the long run is to attack it at its roots—by improving the health, out-of-school environment, and precollegiate education of disadvantaged students who suffer the vicissitudes of urban and rural poverty. But in the meantime, there is more that can be done at the college level to close the gap between underrepresented minorities and other students in both educational and life outcomes.

Some have suggested that income- or class-based admissions preferences could, in fact, replace race-conscious admissions. In the simulations that we did for our book, low-income students are given the same admissions advantage as legacy students and underrepresented minority groups retain their current degree of admissions advantage. The admissions probability for low-income candidates at the schools in our study could be expected to increase substantially—from 32 percent at present to 47 percent. The admissions probability for all other applicants falls, as it would have to, but only from 39 percent to 38 percent. The explanation is, of course, the relative sizes of the applicant pools. Applying current group-by-SAT enrollment rates, our simulations show that the share of the class comprised of students from low-income families could be expected to increase from 11 percent to about 17 percent. The minority share would (by assumption) stay constant at just over 13 percent, and the share of all other students would decline from 79 to 74 percent.

When we simulated the effects of *income-sensitive* admissions preferences using the same preferences accorded legacy candidates—*but* eliminated *race-sensitive* admissions preferences, we found that the share of students who are minorities fell by nearly half—although African Americans, Hispanics, and Native Americans are disproportionately represented among socioeconomically disadvantaged college applicants, the vast majority of disadvantaged candidates are white.[29]

There are three kinds of potential "costs" associated with this hypothetical "legacy thumb" erosion of the academic profile, a decrease in alumni giving, and increased financial aid costs. For various reasons, only the last of these bears out substantially. We estimate that for our group of private liberal arts colleges, with a average of 500 students per class, grant aid funds would have to increase about $460,000 per class, per year (or just under $2 million for all four classes per year; approximately a 12 percent increase, if current financial aid policies were maintained. For the private universities in our study, with 1,500 students per class, the necessary increase could be expected to be about $1.4 million per class, per year, or between $5 and $6 million for all four classes, which is also approximately a 12 percent increase—not a small amount, but certainly affordable for the 30 or 40 wealthiest colleges and universities in the country.[30]

If enrolling a "critical mass" of minority students is a goal of higher education and society—as the overwhelming support for the University of Michigan in *Grutter* from other universities and the corporate and military establishment, generally, would seem to indicate—then income-based preferences are not a sufficient substitute for race-based preferences.

In our opinion, equity cannot be achieved through a need-blind admissions approach that was designed a half-century ago when higher education was much more restricted to an elite clientele than it is today. Treating qualified students from low-SES and low-parental education backgrounds exactly the same as all other applicants gives insufficient weight to the accomplishments of students who have "bucked the odds" by making it into the credible applicant pool.

Finally, in conclusion: If America's leading colleges and universities are to become genuine agents of social mobility and economic opportunity, complementing affirmative action with a "**thumb on the scale**" for academically qualified but socioeconomically disadvantaged students would seem to be an excellent next step and a practical and effective complement to race-based preferences.

This keynote address is based on excerpts from our forthcoming book: William G. Bowen, Martin A. Kurzweil, and Eugene M. Tobin, *Equity and Excellence in American Higher Education* (Charlottesville, Va: University of Virginia Press, 2005).

Endnotes

1. "Ever Higher Society, Ever Harder to Ascend," *Economist* (January 1–7, 2005): 22–24.

2. William Safire, *Lend Me Your Ears: Great Speeches in History* (New York: W.W. Norton & Company, 1992), 21.

3. See Jeffrey Selingo, "U.S. Public's Confidence in Colleges Remains High," *Chronicle of Higher Education* (May 7, 2004) online edition; and John Immerwahr, *Public Attitudes on Higher Education: A Trend Analysis, 1993 to 2003*, prepared by Public Agenda for the National Center for Public Policy and Higher Education, February 2004.

4. Selingo (2004).

5. For a fuller historical treatment of these issues, see William G. Bowen, Martin A. Kurzweil, and Eugene M. Tobin, *Equity and Excellence in American Higher Education* (Charlottesville, Va.: University of Virginia Press, 2005), chapter 2.

6. Samuel Eliot Morison, *Three Centuries of Harvard, 1636–1936* (Cambridge, Mass.: Belknap Press of Harvard University Press, 1965), 199.

7. Harold S. Wechsler, *The Qualified Student: A History of Selective College Admission in America* (New York: Wiley, 1977), 66.

8. Geoffrey Kabaservice, *The Guardians: Kingman Brewster, His Circle, and the Rise of the Liberal Establishment* (New York: Henry Holt, 2004), 259, 261, 263–272.

9. *Trends in College Pricing*, (College Board, 2003). Only 54 percent of high school graduates from the lowest income quartile enroll in college, compared to 82 percent of those with incomes above $88,675 [the top quartile].

10. See Bowen, Kurzweil, and Tobin, *Equity and Excellence in American Higher Education*, chapter 4.

11. Richard D. Kahlenberg, *America's Untapped Resource: Low-Income Students in Higher Education* (New York: The Century Foundation Press, 2004), 16.

12. Pedro Carneiro and James Heckman, "Human Capital Policy," in James J. Heckman and Alan B. Krueger, *Inequality in America: What Role for Human Capital Policies?* (Cambridge, Mass.: MIT Press, 2003), 119.

13. See Bowen, Kurzweil, and Tobin, *Equity and Excellence in American Higher Education*, chapter 4.

14. See Clifford Adelman, *Principal Indicators of Student Academic Histories in Postsecondary Education, 1972–2000* (Washington, D.C.: U.S. Department of Education, Institute of Education Sciences, 2004), table 3.1.

15. These calculations are based on 2000 U.S. Census data prepared by Sarah Turner and delivered in personal correspondence August 15, 2004.

16. Sarah E. Turner, "Going to College and Finishing College: Explaining Different Educational Outcomes," in Caroline Hoxby, ed., *College Choices: The Economics of Where to Go, When to Go, and How to Pay for It* (Chicago, Ill.: University of Chicago Press, 2004).

17. Turner (2004), 1–2.

18. The schools in this special study include five Ivy League universities (Columbia, Harvard, Princeton, the University of Pennsylvania, and Yale), ten academically selective liberal arts colleges (Barnard, Bowdoin, Macalester, Middlebury, Oberlin, Pomona, Smith, Swarthmore, Wellesley, and Williams), and four leading state universities (The Pennsylvania State University, the University of California-Los Angeles, the University of Illinois at Urbana/Champaign, and the University of Virginia).

19. See Steven Ruggles and Matthew Sobek et al., Integrated Public Use Microdata Series: Version 3.0 (Minneapolis: Historical Census Projects, University of Minnesota, 2003), http://www.ipums.org.

20. These estimates are consistent with the data in Anthony P. Carnevale and Stephen J. Rose, "Socioeconomic Status, Race/Ethnicity, and Selective College Admissions," in Richard D. Kahlenberg, ed., *America's Untapped Resource: Low-Income Students in Higher Education* (New York: Century Foundation Press, 2004), 101–156.

21. The share of the national population of teenagers whose parents had not attended college and whose family income placed them in the bottom quartile in 1992 is determined by the authors' (Bowen, Kurzweil, and Tobin) analyses using data drawn from the National Center for Education Statistics' National Educational Longitudinal Study (NELS) of 1988 eighth-graders.

22. See Bowen, Kurzweil, and Tobin, *Equity and Excellence in American Higher Education*, chapter 5.

23. Data reported by David Leonhardt of the *New York Times* suggest that the socioeconomically advantaged character of the student bodies of the four public institutions in our study is typical of the student bodies of selective public institutions across the country. He reports that "at the 42 most selective state universities, including the flagship campuses in California, Colorado, Illinois, Michigan, and New York, 40 percent of [2003-04] freshmen come from families making more than $100,000," according to the Higher Education Research Institute, which publishes the American freshmen survey. (Leonhardt, "As Wealthy Fill Top Colleges, Concerns Grow Over Fairness," *New York Times* [April 22, 2004]: A1, A21.)

24. See Bowen, Kurzweil, and Tobin, *Equity and Excellence in American Higher Education*, chapter 5.

25. In general, the patterns are very similar but there are a few small differences. The public institutions in our (Bowen, Kurzweil, Tobin) study give a modest adjusted advantage to applicants from low-income families (about 5 percentage points), even though the private schools do not. On the other hand, the private colleges give more of a boost to first-generation applicants than do public institutions (an adjusted admissions advantage of 4.3 points at private colleges versus 2.0 at the publics). The most substantial difference between the admissions practices of public and private institutions is in the awarding of a legacy preference. At the private institutions, the adjusted admissions advantage for legacies is about 21 percentage points, while the public institutions provide legacies with only a 5.5 percentage point advantage. The adjusted admissions advantages for recruited athletes are roughly 31 points at both public and private institutions—though it must be remembered that with their higher "base" admissions percentage, this means that the public institutions are admitting recruited athletes at a much higher rate (about 82 percent versus 62 percent for the private institutions). Finally, minority preferences are about 6 points higher at the public universities than at the private institutions (30.6 points versus 25.1).

26. William G. Bowen and Derek Bok, *The Shape of the River: Long-Term Consequences of Considering Race in College and University Admissions* (Princeton, N.J.: Princeton University Press, 1998), 76–90; and William G. Bowen and Sarah A. Levin, *Reclaiming the Game: College Sports and Educational Values* (Princeton, N.J.: Princeton University Press, 2003), 235–240.

27. For a detailed discussion of the competing demands in providing admissions preferences for special groups, see Bowen, Kurzweil, and Tobin, *Equity and Excellence in American Higher Education*, chapter 7.

28. See James L. Shulman and William G. Bowen, *The Game of Life: College Sports and Educational Values* (Princeton, N.J.: Princeton University Press, 2000); and Bowen and Levin, *Reclaiming the Game.*

29. See Bowen, Kurzweil, and Tobin, *Equity and Excellence in American Higher Education*, chapter 7.

30. These calculations were made based on the income distribution, net price by income, and list tuition of institutions in the Consortium on Financing Higher Education reported by Catharine Hill, Gordon Winston, and Stephanie Boyd in "Affordability: Family Incomes and Net Prices at Highly Selective Private Colleges and Universities," Williams College Project on the Economics of Higher Education, Discussion Paper no. 66 (October 2003) 5, 8.

Appendix B

List of Participants

John Albright Chief Educational Manager, Higher Education	The College Board	jalbright@collegeboard.org
Photo Anagnostopoulos Senior Vice President, Product Development	The College Board	photoa@collegeboard.org
Diane Anci Dean of Admission	Mount Holyoke College	danci@mtholyoke.edu
David Armstrong Chancellor	Florida Community Colleges & Workforce Education	david.armstrong@fldoe.org
Ben Baglio Consultant	Cold Spring Harbor High School	asop@optonline.net
Cynthia Bailey Executive Director, Education FInance, CUES	The College Board	cbailey@collegeboard.org
Gretchen Bataille Senior Vice President of Academic Affairs	University of North Carolina at Chapel Hill	bataille@northcarolina.edu
Mary Lou W. Bates Dean of Admissions & Financial Aid	Skidmore College	mbates@skidmore.edu
James M. Bauer Assistant Dean of Enrollment	University of Miami	jbauer@miami.edu
Sandy Baum Senior Policy Analyst	The College Board	sbaum@collegeboard.org
John Baworowsky Vice President	Saint Louis University	johnb@slu.edu
Wendy Beckemeyer Vice President, Enrollment	Alfred University	beckemeyer@alfred.edu
Jacquelyn Belcher President	Georgia Perimeter College	jbelcher@gpc.edu
Andre Bell Vice President, College & University Enrollment Services	The College Board	abell@collegeboard.org
James Belvin, Jr. Director of Financial Aid	Duke University	jim.belvin@duke.edu
Jocelyn Bennett Director of Scholarships & Special Programs	The Pennsylvania State University	jmb15@psu.edu
Julia Benz Director of Student Financial Services	Rice University	benz@rice.edu
Gail Berson Dean of Admission & Student Aid	Wheaton College	gberson@wheatoncollege.edu
Don Betterton Director of Financial Aid	Princeton University	dbett@princeton.edu
Cheryl Blanco Senior Program Director, Policy Analysis & Research	Western Interstate Commission for Higher Education	cblanco@wiche.edu

Patricia Bogart Senior Associate Director of Undergraduate Financial Aid	Duke University	pat.bogart@duke.edu
William Boyd Associate Vice President, Student Services	San Diego State University	jbarnum@mail.sdsu.edu
Antonio Boyle Director of Admissions	Alabama A&M University	antonio.boyle@email.aamu.edu
John Brady Chief Educational Manager, Higher Education	The College Board	jbrady@collegeboard.org
Sharon Brennan Director of Admissions & Enrollment	Southern Connecticut State University	brennan@southernct.edu
Steven Brooks Executive Director	North Carolina State Education Assistance Authority	sbrooks@ncseaa.edu
Jane Brown Vice President for Enrollment & College Relations	Mount Holyoke College	jbbrown@mtholyoke.edu
Charles Bruce Senior Director, Office of Scholarships & Financial Aid	Oklahoma State University	charles.bruce@okstate.edu
Jonathan Burdick Dean of Admissions & Financial Aid	University of Rochester	deanafa@rochester.edu
Kristine Butz Associate Director of Financial Aid	Butler University	kbutz@butler.edu
Nancy Cable Vice President & Dean of Admissions & Financial Aid	Davidson College	nacable@davidson.edu
Paul Calme Director of Financial Aid	Xavier University	calme@xavier.edu
Wayne Camara Vice President, Research & Product Development	The College Board	wcamara@collegeboard.org
Marc Camille Dean of Admission	Xavier University	camille@xavier.edu
Gaston Caperton President	The College Board	gcaperton@collegeboard.org
William Carswell Manager, Scholarships & Grants	North Carolina State Education Assistance Authority	carswellb@ncseaa.edu
Robin Casanova Program Associate, Financial Aid Services	The College Board	rcasanova@collegeboard.org
Joe Paul Case Dean & Director of Financial Aid	Amherst College	jpcase@amherst.edu
Arlene Cash Vice President	Spelman College	acash@spelman.edu
Dave Cecil Director of Financial Aid	Transylvania University	dcecil@transy.edu
Vicky Centeno Executive Assistant, Office of the Secretary	The College Board	vcenteno@collegeboard.org

Debra Chermonte Dean of Admissions & Financial Aid	Oberlin College	debra.chermonte@oberlin.edu
Martha Childress College Counselor	St. John's School	mchildress@sjs.org
Douglas Christiansen Assistant Vice President for Enrollment Management	Purdue University	dlchristiansen@purdue.edu
Elizabeth Cittadine Director, College Bridge	Chicago Public Schools	bcittadine@cps.k12.il.us
Art Coleman Attorney	Holland and Knight, LLP	arthur.coleman@hklaw.com
Karen Cooper Associate Dean & Director of Financial Aid	Stanford University	karen.cooper@stanford.edu
Youlonda Copeland-Morgan Associate Vice President of Admission & Financial Aid	Harvey Mudd College	youlanda_copelandmorgan@hmc.edu
Kevin Coveney Vice President, Enrollment	Washington College	kcoveney2@washcoll.edu
Patricia A. Coye Director of Financial Aid	Pomona College	pac04747@pomona.edu
Linda Dagradi Director of Guidance	Longmeadow High School	ldagradi@longmeadow.k12.ma.us
Lisa Dawkins College Counselor	Evangelical Christian School	lmdawkins@esceagles.com
Charles Deacon Dean of Admissions	Georgetown University	deacon@georgetown.edu
Anne Deahl Associate Provost for Enrollment	Marquette University	anne.deahl@marquette.edu
John DeCourcy Director of Financial Aid	Washington & Lee University	jdecourcy@wlu.edu
Arlina DeNardo Director of Financial Aid	Lafayette College	denardoa@lafayette.edu
Jennifer Desjarlais Dean of Admission	Wellesley College	jdesjarl@wellesley.edu
Georgette DeVeres Associate Vice President, Admissions and Financial Aid	Claremont McKenna College	gdeveres@mckenna.edu
Fred Dietrich Senior Vice President, Higher Education	The College Board	fdietrich@collegeboard.org
Kay Dietrich Educational Manager, Higher Education	The College Board	kdietrich@collegeboard.org
Rebecca Dixon Associate Provost of University Enrollment	Northwestern University	r-dixon@northwestern.edu
Jean Dobson Associate Director, Financial Aid	Emory University	jdobson@emory.edu

Sally Donahue Director of Financial Aid	Harvard College	sdonahue@fas.harvard.edu
Patsy Emery Director, Financial Aid Operations	Northwestern University	pemery@northwestern.edu
Deren Finks Vice President & Dean of Admissions & Financial Aid	Harvey Mudd College	deren_finks@hmc.edu
Bill Fitzsimmons Dean of Admissions & Financial Aid	Harvard University	pacholok@fas.harvard.edu
Adriana Flores Manager, New SAT Outreach	The College Board	aflores@collegeboard.org
Jennifer Fondiller Dean of Admissions	Barnard College	jfondill@barnard.edu
Karen Fooks Director of Student Financial Affairs	University of Florida	kfooks@ufl.edu
Pamela W. Fowler Director of Financial Aid	University of Michigan	pfowler@umich.edu
Michael Fraher Director of Financial Aid	Vassar College	mifraher@vassar.edu
Scott Friedhoff Vice President for Enrollment	Allegheny College	scott.friedhoff@allegheny.edu
Ellen Frishberg University Financial Aid	Johns Hopkins University	efrish@jhu.edu
Clint Gasaway Director of Financial Aid	Wabash College	gasawayc@wabash.edu
Philip Gebauer Director of Admission	Rockhurst University	philip.gebauer@rockhurst.edu
Connie Gores Vice President for Enrollment	Randolph-Macon Women's College	cgores@rmwc.edu
Daniel Goyette Director, Office of Student Financial Aid	Marquette University	dan.goyette@marquette.edu
Steven Graff Senior Consultant & Director of Enrollment	The College Board	sgraff@collegeboard.org
Larry Griffith Assistant Vice President, Middle States Regional Office	The College Board	lgriffith@collegeboard.org
Anna Griswold Assistant Vice Provost for Enrollment	The Pennsylvania State University	amg5@psu.edu
Stephen Handel Director, Community College Initiatives	The College Board	shandel@collegeboard.org
Julia K. Harmon Associate Director, Student Scholarships	University of Dayton	kharmon@udayton.edu
M. Seamus Harreys Dean, Student Financial Services	Northeastern University	s.harreys@neu.edu

L. Katharine Harrington Associate Dean of Admission & Financial Aid	University of Southern California	lkh@usc.edu
William Hartog Dean of Admissions & Financial Aid	Washington & Lee University	bhartog@wlu.edu
Pat Hayashi Senior Fellow	University of California	pat.hayashi@ucop.edu
Don Heller Associate Professor & Senior Research Associate	The Pennsylvania State University	dheller@psu.edu
Ann Hendrick Dean of Admissions & Financial Aid	Millsaps College	hendrag@millsaps.edu
Eric Hinton Admissions Coordinator	New College of Florida	ehinton@ncf.edu
Pamela Horne Assistant to Provost for Enrollment	Michigan State University	pamhorne@msu.edu
William H. Hurry Executive Director	Rhode Island Higher Education Assistance Authority	whurry@riheaa.org
Henry Ingle Associate Vice President, Office of Technology, Planning and Distance Learning	University of Texas at El Paso	hingle@utep.edu
Monica Inzer Dean of Admission & Financial Aid	Hamilton College	minzer@hamilton.edu
Edward Irish Director, Student Financial Aid	College of William & Mary	epiris@wm.edu
Janet Irons Associate Director of Financial Aid	Harvard College	irons@fas.harvard.edu
Candynce A. Jackson Student Loan Coordinator	University of Miami	cjackson@miami.edu
Mary S. Jemail Director of College Guidance	Convent of the Sacred Heart	mjemail@cshnyc.org
Christina Jensen Associate Director, Financial Aid	Colorado School of Mines	cjensen@mines.edu
Pamela Johnson Vice President for Enrollment	Dominican University	pjohnson@dom.edu
Stephen Joyce Director of Student Aid	Bowdoin College	sjoyce@bowdoin.edu
Michael Kabbaz Senior Educational Manager, Higher Education	The College Board	mkabbaz@collegeboard.org
Eva Kampits Director, Office of the Executive Director	New England Association of Schools & Colleges, Inc. (NEASC)	kampits@neasc.org
Thomas Keane Director, Office of Financial Aid & Student Employment	Cornell University	tck2@cornell.edu
Nancy Kidder Administrative Dean, Enrollment Services	Orange Coast College	nkidder@cccd.edu

Kathleen Killion Dean, Admissions & Financial Aid	New College of Florida	kkillion@ncf.edu
Alan Kines Dean of Undergraduate Admission	Babson College	akines@babson.edu
Roger Koester Director of Financial Aid	Colorado School of Mines	rkoester@mines.edu
Karen Krause Director, Office of Financial Aid	University of Texas at Arlington	kkrause@uta.edu
George La Noue Professor of Political Science	UMBC/Office for Civil Rights, USDOE	glanour@umbc.edu
Rick Lamberson Assistant Director of Admissions	New College of Florida	lamberson@ncf.edu
Jim Lane Director of Student Financial Aid	Texas Tech University	marci.beasley@ttu.edu
John Latting Director of Undergraduate Admissions	Johns Hopkins University	jhiscox1@jhu.edu
Bob Lay Dean of Enrollment Management	Boston College	lay@bc.edu
Mark Lindenmeyer Director of Financial Aid	Loyola College in Maryland	lindenmeyer@loyola.edu
Carolyn Lindley University Director of Financial Aid	Northwestern University	c-lindley@northwestern.edu
Kathleen Little Senior Executive Director, Financial Aid	The College Board	klittle@collegeboard.org
Gilma Lopez Associate Director of Financial Aid	Harvey Mudd College	gilma_lopez@hmc.edu
Mona Lucas Dean of Financial Aid	Cornell University	mll44@cornell.edu
Linda MacRae Associate Director of Admissions	University of North Carolina, Wilmington	macrael@uncw.edu
Douglas Massey Professor of Sociology	Princeton University	dmassey@princeton.edu
Larry Matthews Assistant Vice President, Midwestern Regional Office	The College Board	lmatthews@collegeboard.org
Susan McCrackin Director, PROFILE & Need Analysis	The College Board	smccrackin@collegeboard.org
Christine McGuire Director of Financial Assistance	Boston University	chmcguir@bu.edu
Joann McKenna Vice President for Enrollment	Bentley College	jmckenna@bentley.edu
Sam McNair Executive Director, Admission & Enrollment	The College Board	smcnair@collegeboard.org
Barbara McVicker Coordinator, LD Testing	St. John's School	bmcvicker@sjs.org

Patricia McWade Dean of Student Financial Services	Georgetown University	mcwadep@georgetown.edu
Thomas McWhertor Vice President for Enrollment & External Relations	Calvin College	mcwhto@calvin.edu
Nancy Hargrave Meislahn Dean of Admission & Financial Aid	Wesleyan University	nmeislahn@wesleyan.edu
Joseph Merante Associate Vice President for Academic Affairs	Loyola Marymount University	jmerante@lmu.edu
Jim Miller Dean, Admissions & Financial Aid	Bowdoin College	jmiller3@bowdoin.edu
Dolores Mize Associate Vice Chancellor	Oklahoma State Regents for Higher Education	dmize@osrhe.edu
David Mohning Director of Student Financial Aid & Asst., Prof.	Vanderbilt University	d.mohning@vanderbilt.edu
Nancy Monnich Vice President for Enrollment	Beloit College	monnich@beloit.edu
James Montoya Vice President for Regions & Higher Education Services	The College Board	jmontoya@collegeboard.org
Melissa Moser Director, Financial Aid	Orange Coast College	mmoser@mail.occ.cccd.edu
Warren Muller Dean of Admissions, Marketing & Communications	Albertson College of Idaho	wmuller@albertson.edu
Chris Munoz Vice Provost for Enrollment	Case Western Reserve University	chris.munoz@case.edu
Jeani Narcum Director of Office of Student Aid	Washington College	jnarcum2@washcoll.edu
Dan Nelson Senior Director of Financial Aid	Bethel University	de-nelson@bethel.edu
Lynn Nichelson Director of Financial Aid	Illinois Wesleyan University	lnichels@iwu.edu
Mary Nucciarone Assistant Director of Financial Aid	University of Notre Dame	mnucciar@nd.edu
Erica O'Neal Assistant Vice President of Student Affairs	California Institute of Technology	eoneal@studaff.caltech.edu
Stuart Oremus Director of College Counseling	The Wellington School	oremus@wellington.org
Shirley Ort Associate Provost & Director of Scholarship and Student Aid	University of North Carolina at Chapel Hill	sao@unc.edu
Peter Osgood Director of Admissions	Harvey Mudd College	Peter_Osgood@hmc.edu
Rodney Oto Associate Dean of Admissions & Director of Student Financial Services	Carleton College	roto@acs.carleton.edu

Julia Padgett Director, Financial Aid	Emory University	jperrea@emory.edu
Raymund Paredes Commissioner	Texas Higher Education Coordinating Board	raymund.paredes@thecb.state. tx.us
Tom Parker Dean of Admission & Financial Aid	Amherst College	thparter@amherst.edu
Abby Parsons Associate Director of Financial Aid	California Institute of Technology	aparsons@finaid.caltech.edu
Linda Peckham Director of Training & Communications	The College Board	lpeckham@collegeboard.edu
Bernie Pekala Director of Student Financial Strategies	Boston College	pekala@bc.edu
Bruce Poch Vice President & Dean of Admissions	Pomona College	bruce.poch@pomona.edu
Anna Marie Porras Director of Admission	Stanford University	aporras@stanford.edu
Charles W. Puls Director of Financial Aid	University of Rochester	cpuls@finaid.rochester.edu
Stephen Pultz Director of Admissions	University of San Diego	spultz@sandiego.edu
Lane Ramey Director of Freshmen Admission	Rockhurst University	lane.ramey@rockhurst.edu
Robin Randall Assistant Vice President of Enrollment	Wheaton College	rrandall@wheatoncollege.edu
Janet Rapelye Dean of Admission	Princeton University	jrapelye@princeton.edu
Patricia Reilly Director of Financial Aid	Tufts University	patricia.reilly@tufts.edu
Sandra Riley Associate Director, Public Affairs	The College Board	sriley@collegeboard.org
Margaret Robinson Coordinator of Admissions	New College of Florida	mrobinson@ncf.edu
Lorne Robinson Dean of Admissions & Financial Aid	Macalester College	robinson@macalester.edu
Tom Rudin Vice President, Government Relations	The College Board	trudin@collegeboard.org
Joseph Russo Director, Office of Student Financial Services	University of Notre Dame	russo.4@nd.edu
Peter Sacks Speaker		psacks@cableone.net
Judy Sakaki Vice Chancellor of Student Affairs	University of California: Davis	jsakaki@ucdavis.edu
Don Saleh Associate Vice President of Enrollment Management	Syracuse University	dasaleh@syr.edu

Martha Salmon Assistant Vice President, Southwestern Regional Office	The College Board	msalmon@collegeboard.org
Mary San Agustin Director of Financial Aid & Scholarships	Palomar College	msanagustin@palomar.edu
Mayten Sanchez Director of Admissions	Bloomfield College	mayten_sanchez@bloomfield.edu
Daniel Saracino Assistant Provost for Enrollment	University of Notre Dame	saracino.3@nd.edu
William Schilling Director of Student Financial Aid	University of Pennsylvania	schilling@sfs.upenn.edu
Deb Thyng Schmidt Consultant	The College Board	dtsco@msn.com
Michael Schoenfeld Vice President for College Advancement	Middlebury College	schoenfe@middlebury.edu
Michael Scott Director of Scholarships & Financial Aid	Texas Christian University	m.scott@tcu.edu
Mary Carroll Scott Vice President, Membership	The College Board	mcscott@collegeboard.org
Dorothy Sexton Secretary of the Corporation	The College Board	dsexton@collegeboard.edu
Anne Shea Vice President for Enrollment & Student Affairs	Boston University	ashea@bu.edu
Ellen Shilkret Associate Director, Financial Aid	Vassar College	elshilkret@vassar.edu
Joellen Silberman Dean of Enrollment	Kalamazoo College	silbermn@kzoo.edu
Cindy Skaruppa Associate Provost	Our Lady of the Lake University	skarc@lake.ollusa.edu
James Slattery Chief Educational Manager, Higher Education	The College Board	jslattery@collegeboard.org
Audrey Smith Dean of Enrollment	Smith College	aysmith@smith.edu
Peter Stace Vice President for Enrollment	Fordham University	stace@fordham.edu
Elizabeth Stanley Chief Educational Manager, Higher Education	The College Board	estanley@collegeboard.org
Kathleen Stevenson Senior Associate Dean of Admission & Financial Aid	Davidson College	kastevenson@davidson.edu
Forrest Stuart Director of Financial Aid	Rhodes College	stuart@rhodes.edu
Anne Sturtevant Director, Financial Aid Solutions	The College Board	asturtevant@collegeboard.org

Randy Swing Co-Director & Senior Scholar	Policy Center on the First Year of College	swing@fyfoundations.org
Laura Talbot Director of Financial Aid	Swarthmore College	ltalbot1@swarthmore.edu
Nanci Tessier Vice President for Enrollment	Saint Anselm College	ntessier@anselm.edu
Catherine C. Thomas Associate Dean of Enrollment Services	University of Southern California	ccthomas@usc.edu
J. Michael Thompson Vice Provost for Enrollment Management	University of Southern California	vpenroll@use.edu
Eugene Tobin Program Officer in Higher Education for the Liberal Arts College Program	The Andrew W. Mellon Foundation	emt@mellon.org
Marcelle Tyburski Director of Financial Aid	Colgate University	mtyburski@mail.colgate.edu
Frank Valines Associate Director, Office of Student Financial Aid	University of Maryland	fvalines@umd.edu
Chauncey Veatch Teacher	Coachella Valley High School	cveatch@coachella.k12.ca.us
Kelly Walter Executive Director of Admissions	Boston University	kwalter@bu.edu
Ann-Marie Waterman Senior Educational Manager	The College Board	awaterman@collegeboard.org
Gary Weaver Associate Director of Student Aid	Bowdoin College	gweaver@bowdoin.edu
William Wells Director of Financial Aid	Wake Forest University	wellswt@wfu.edu
Patricia White College Counselor	Summit Country Day	white_p@summitcds.org
Lucia Whittelsey Director of Financial Aid	Colby College	lwwhitte@colby.edu
Ken Woods Chief Educational Manager, Western Regional Office	The College Board	kwoods@collegeboard.org
Ann Wright Vice President for Enrollment	Rice University	awright@rice.edu
Sonia Wu Assistant Director of Admissions	New College of Florida	swu@ncf.edu
Bill Young Associate Vice President & Director of Enrollment/Financial Aid Office	Colorado School of Mines	wyoung@mines.edu
Alan Young Dean of Enrollment Management	Marlboro College	ayoung@marlboro.edu
Kristine Zavoli Acting Assistant Vice President	The College Board	kzavoli@collegeboard.org

Appendix C

College Scholarship Service Council 2004–2005

Youlonda Copeland-Morgan, Chair
Associate Vice President of Admission
and Financial Aid
Harvey Mudd College

Shirley A. Ort, Chair-Elect
Associate Provost and Director of
Scholarships and Student Aid
University of North Carolina at Chapel Hill

William Schilling, Past Chair
Director of Student Financial Aid
University of Pennsylvania

Steven E. Brooks
Executive Director
North Carolina State Education
Assistance Authority

Julia Benz
Director, Student Financial Services
Rice University

Arlene Cash
Vice President for Enrollment
Management
Spelman College

Micaela Connery
Advisory Panel Student
Fordham College of Liberal Studies

Carroll Davis
Coordinator for College Counseling
North Central High School (IN)

Arlina DeNardo
Director of Financial Aid
Lafayette College

Clinton Gasaway
Director of Financial Aid
Wabash College

Matthew W. Hamilton
Registrar and Associate Vice President for
Enrollment and Student Financial Aid
University of Oklahoma

M. Seamus Harreys
Dean, Student Financial Services
Northeastern University

Mark Lindenmeyer
Director of Financial Aid
Loyola College in Maryland

Lidia Lyman
Guidance Counselor
White Plains High School (NY)

James Malloy
Associate Director, Student
Financial Aid Services
University of Notre Dame

Ronald S. Martinez
Director of Financial Aid
University of New Mexico

Rhonda McKinnon
Assistant Vice President/Executive Director
for Student and Community Programs
Cuyahoga Community College

Kyle L. Mitchell
Advisory Panel Student
Yale University

Eileen O'Leary
Assistant Vice President for Finance/
Director, Student Aid and Finance
Stonehill College

Julia Padgett
Director of Financial Aid
Emory University

Bryan Terry
Director, Financial Aid
Florida Agricultural and Mechanical University

Catherine C. Thomas
Associate Dean of Enrollment Services/
Director of Financial Aid
University of Southern California

William T. Wells
Director of Financial Aid
Wake Forest University

Charlotte Winkelmann
Assistant Director, Student
Support Services
Austin Independent School District (TX)

Appendix D

College Scholarship Service Council Financial Aid Standards and Services Committee

Mary Nucciarone, Chair
Assistant Director of Financial Aid
University of Notre Dame

Sally Donahue, Vice-Chair
Director of Financial Aid
Harvard College

Julia Benz
Director of Student Financial Services
Rice University

Pamela W. Fowler
Director of Financial Aid
University of Michigan

Cynthia Hartley
Director of Graduate Student Aid Programs
Stanford University

Stanley G. Hudson
Associate Dean for Student Services
Harvard School of Public Health

Mark Lindenmeyer
Director of Financial Aid
Loyola College in Maryland

Rodney M. Oto
Director of Student Financial Services and
Associate Dean of Admissions
Carleton College

Julia Padgett
Director of Financial Aid
Emory University

Marcelle Tyburski
Director of Financial Aid
Colgate University